Walk Around

F-86 Sabre

By Larry Davis

Color by Don Greer and Richard Hudson

Illustrated by Richard Hudson

Walk Around Number 21

squadron/signal publications

Introduction

SABREJET — Just the word brings to mind thoughts of silver, swept-wing jet fighters wheeling and zooming in the cold blue skies over northwest Korea. The North American F-86 Sabre was the western world's premier fighter aircraft during the early 1950s. To many of the Communist pilots that were competing against the F-86 in 'MiG Alley,' the Sabre was also better than anything flying in the eastern world. Over 800 MiG pilots in Korea discovered first-hand about the superiority of the F-86.

The F-86, however, did not begin its life as the premier fighter design of its time. The design began during the waning years of World War Two, when the Allies were engaging the jet aircraft of Hitler's Luftwaffe. The Messerschmitt Me 262, powered by two Junkers Jumo 004B jet engines, was 90 miles (144.8 KM) per hour faster than the best Allied fighter, the Supermarine Spitfire Mk. XIV. Only stupidity on the part of the Nazi leaders kept the Me 262 from wresting air superiority away from the propeller-driven Allied fighters that had worked so long and hard to win it.

Propeller aircraft were doomed by the introduction of the Me 262. Even the vaunted North American P-51 Mustang and de Havilland Mosquito were no match for the speed of the German jets. The Allies began crash programs to put their own jets into the air. Engineers at North American Aviation designed a new aircraft designated the XP-86, the planform of which bore some resemblance to the earlier P-51 Mustang.

The straight-wing XP-86 jet fighter, although equal to the speed of the Luftwaffe's Me 262, did not have the speed that the US Army Air Forces planners had hoped for. Additionally, neither the Lockheed P-80 Shooting Star, already in production, nor the Republic XP-84 Thunderjet possessed the range of speed desired by the USAAF. Something else was needed in the XP-86 design to make the aircraft the fighter that everyone thought a jet could be. That 'something' was the swept wing.

In late 1945, after considerable development of the straight wing design had been underway, North American engineers decided to mate a swept wing to the existing XP-86 airframe design. Wind tunnel testing revealed astonishing results. These results indicated an aircraft capable of flying at or near the speed of sound — Mach One (approximately 670 MPH (1078 KMH) at 30,000 feet (9144 M). The swept-wing XP-86 would be able to fly at speeds almost 150 MPH (241 KMH) faster than other jet fighter designs of the era.

The Army Air Force gave the go-ahead to the redesign of the XP-86 on 20 November 1945. The swept wing XP-86 was rolled out of the North American factory on 8 August 1947. George Welch brought the XP-86 near Mach One on the very first test flight on 1 October 1947. Some aviation historians now contend that Welch may have broken the sound barrier in the XP-86 before Chuck Yeager did so in the Bell X-1 on 14 October 1947.

The die had been cast. The North American P-86 — redesignated F-86 in 1948 — would be built to fulfill four major roles before production ended. These missions included a fighter interceptor, a fighter-bomber, the fastest photo reconnaissance aircraft of its era, and the first single seat, all-weather jet interceptor in history. Eleven variants of the F-86 would be built in five nations around the world, not including license-built overseas sub-variants. The US Navy even purchased a Sabre variant for the fleet, the FJ Fury. Sabres would serve in no less than 31 nations before finally being phased out of service during the late 1980s.

F-86s were pitted against the best fighter in the Communist world — the MiG-15 — during the Korean War. Although similar in design, the MiG-15 was 3310 pounds (1501.4 KG) lighter than the F-86A. F-86 development throughout the war brought the Sabre closer to the MiG-15 in terms of performance. The inexperienced MiG pilots were also no match for the veteran USAF Sabre pilots. By the end of the Korean War, over 800 MiGs had been shot down by F-86 pilots compared to a loss of only 78 F-86s. The kill ratio was an astonishing 10:1 — and some historians state this ratio might be much higher.

In the skies over 'MiG Alley,' the North American F-86 Sabre proved itself to be the finest fighter aircraft design of its era.

ISBN 0-89747-409-0

If you have any photographs of aircraft, armor, soldiers or ships of any nation, particularly wartime snapshots, why not share them with us and help make Squadron/Signal's books all the more interesting and complete in the future. Any photograph sent to us will be copied and the original returned. The donor will be fully credited for any photos used. Please send them to:

Squadron/Signal Publications, Inc.
1115 Crowley Drive
Carrollton, TX 75011-5010

Если у вас есть фотографии самолётов, вооружения, солдат или кораблей любой страны, особенно, снимки времён войны, поделитесь с нами и помогите сделать новые книги издательства Эскадрон/Сигнал ещё интереснее. Мы переснимем ваши фотографии и вернём оригиналы. Имена приславших снимки будут сопровождать все опубликованные фотографии. Пожалуйста, присылайте фотографии по адресу:

Squadron/Signal Publications, Inc.
1115 Crowley Drive
Carrollton, TX 75011-5010

軍用機、装甲車両、兵士、軍艦などの写真を所持しておられる方はいらっしゃいませんか？どの国のものでも結構です。作戦中に撮影されたものが特に良いのです。Squadron/Signal社の出版する刊行物において、このような写真は内容を一層充実し、興味深くすることができます。当方にお送り頂いた写真は、複写の後お返しいたします。出版物中に写真を使用した場合は、必ず提供者のお名前を明記させて頂きます。お写真は下記にご送付ください。

Squadron/Signal Publications, Inc.
1115 Crowley Drive
Carrollton, TX 75011-5010

(Front Cover) BEAUTIOUS BUTCH II was an F-86F flown by Captain Joseph McConnell in the 39th Fighter Interceptor Squadron based at Suwon AB, Korea during 1953. Capt McConnell was the top scoring ace in Korea with 16 MiG kills.

(Previous Page) A flight of F-86Fs assigned to the 25th Fighter Interceptor Squadron (FIS) cruises over 'MiG Alley' in northwest Korea during the first half of 1953. (Keith Johnson)

(Back Cover) Major W.W. 'Bones' Marshall flew F-86E MR. BONES V when he commanded the 335th Fighter Interceptor Squadron at K-14 during the last half of 1951.

The XP-86 used a wing and tail assembly derived from the propeller-driven P-51 Mustang attached to a new fuselage designed around the General Electric J35 axial-flow jet engine. This is the only known photo of the XP-86 mockup. (NAA)

The F-86A was the first production version of the Sabre and became operational in February of 1949. The early F-86As had small electrically operated doors over the gun ports. This F-86A-5, assigned to the 1st Fighter Group (FG) at March AFB, California in 1949, carries 206.5-gallon (781.7 liter) underwing ferry tanks. (Roger Besecker)

XP-86 Evolution

The F-86F was the final development of the basic airframe design. The F-86F featured a more powerful engine and a new, larger swept wing without leading edge slats. This wing was known as the '6-3 hard wing.' The leading edge of this wing was extended six inches (15.2 CM) at the wing root and three inches (7.6 CM) at the wing tip. North American built a total of 2540 F-86Fs. These F-86Fs line the ramp at the North American plant at Inglewood, California. (via Peter Bowers)

XP-86 Straight Wing

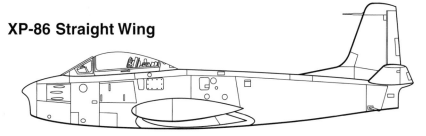

XP-86 Swept Wing

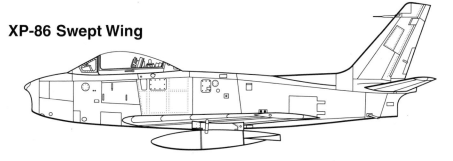

3

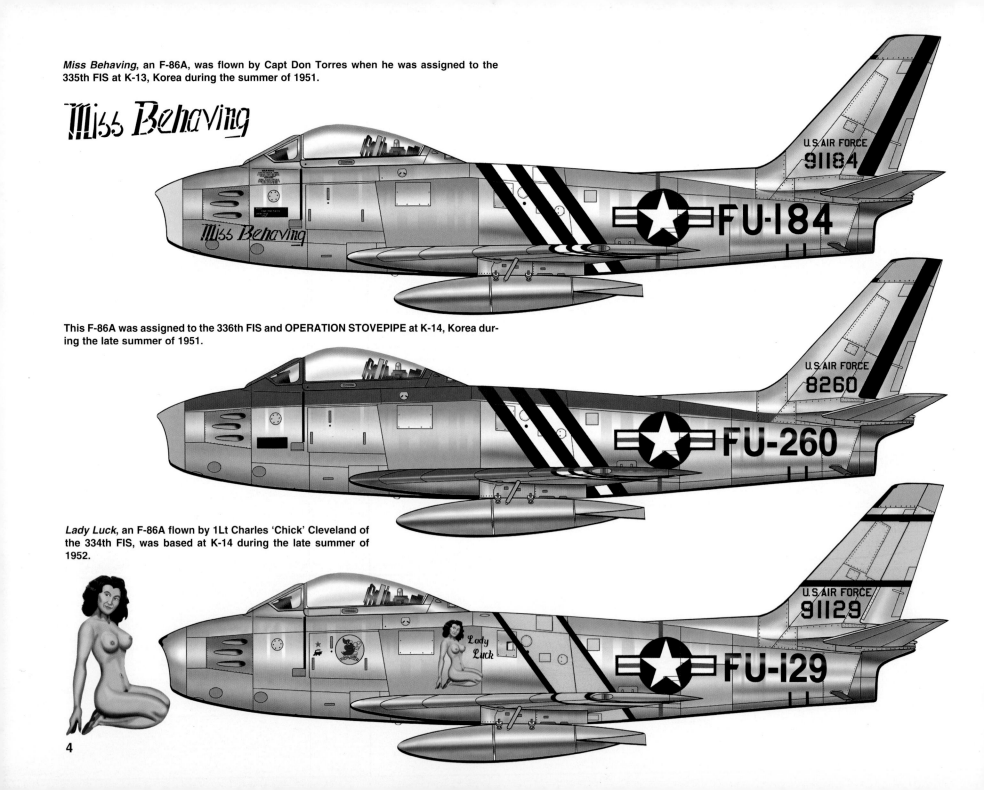

Miss Behaving, an F-86A, was flown by Capt Don Torres when he was assigned to the 335th FIS at K-13, Korea during the summer of 1951.

This F-86A was assigned to the 336th FIS and OPERATION STOVEPIPE at K-14, Korea during the late summer of 1951.

Lady Luck, an F-86A flown by 1Lt Charles 'Chick' Cleveland of the 334th FIS, was based at K-14 during the late summer of 1952.

4

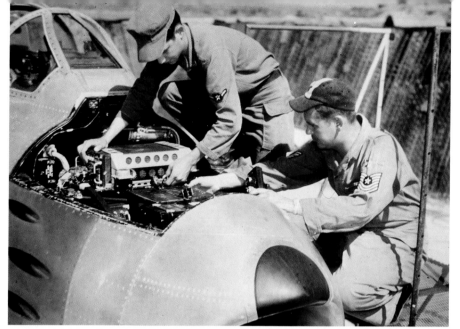

(Above) A pair of 4th Fighter Interceptor Group (FIG) mechanics work on the AN/APG-30 radar assembly. This radar was the heart of the F-86 fire control system. The AN/APG-30 had a range of approximately 3000 yards (2743 M), although it was rarely effective at that range. (USAF)

(Below) Liza Gal/El Diablo was an F-86E flown by Major Chuck Owens of the 336th Fighter Interceptor Squadron (FIS) at K-14 Air Base, Korea in 1952. Although the F-86F was the best of the Sabre variants, it was the F-86E that scored most of the victories in Korea. Major Owens' aircraft shows markings signifying eight MiG kills and fourteen truck kills. (Wm. K. Thomas)

(Above) The F-86 was designed with maintenance in mind and most of the major maintenance areas had completely removable panels for ready access. This F-86F fighter-bomber was assigned to the 67th Fighter Bomber Squadron (FBS) at K-55, Korea in 1953. (James Gregg)

F-86As were equipped with electrically operated gun doors. These gun doors opened in 1/20th of a second when the trigger was pulled. It was later found that the doors froze at the F-86's operating altitudes — often above 45,000 feet (13,716 meters). The doors were either removed or wired open in Korea. The open ammunition bay door served as a step to the cockpit. (NAA)

A 4th FIG crew chief refills the main fuel tank on one of the OPERATION STOVEPIPE F-86As. These Sabres were used for weather reconnaissance flights in Korea during 1951. The upper surfaces have been painted Olive Drab to hide the Sabre from the higher flying MiGs, however, this reduced the F-86's top speed by over 20 MPH (32.2 KMH). This F-86A (48-260) now resides in the Smithsonian National Air and Space Museum. (Al Lukza)

Crewmembers examine the nose wheel assembly of an F-86A assigned to the 71st Fighter Squadron (FS) in 1949. The nose wheel assembly consisted of the early six-spoked Bendix wheel and a six-ply high pressure tire. The forward nose door folded for tire clearance. (NAA)

Radar Bay

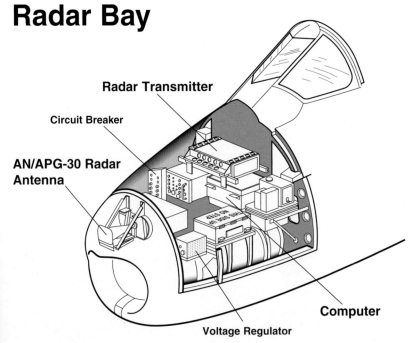

Radar Transmitter

Circuit Breaker

AN/APG-30 Radar Antenna

Computer

Voltage Regulator

(Above) One of a handful of F-86As that are still flying is #48-178, which is owned by Golden Apple Trust in England. 'Ol' 178' is the oldest flying Sabre in the world and is restored in markings of the 4th FIG in Korea. A restored MiG-15 is parked in the background. (Keith Melville)

(Right) A 4th FIG radar technician makes adjustments to the AN/APG-30 ranging radar in Lt Col Glenn Eagleston's F-86A at K-14 in August of 1951. The upper nose compartment contained the transmitter and ranging computer of the AN/APG-30. The radar antenna was located behind the small black radome on the upper lip of the intake. The small square on the lower intake lip is a gun camera port. (USAF)

(Below) The oldest surviving combat veteran of the Korean War is #48-260, which flew with the 4th FIG in Korea. This F-86A is now part of the Smithsonian's National Air and Space Museum collection. The aircraft has been restored to the same markings it carried in early 1951, complete with black and white ID bands. The display also includes pierced steel planking (PSP), which was used for the parking ramps at both Suwon and Kimpo airfields. (Carolyn Russo)

Crew chiefs from the 51st FIG turn MISS B, an F-86E, on the alert ramp at K-13 during the first half of 1952. The nose intake ring is brown natural fiberglass. These intakes — also painted light gray — were found on F-86As and early F-86E-1s before being replaced by metal units. (USAF)

Lt Col Herman Vischer of the 25th FIS stands by the nose of his F-86E, HENRIETTA/7 come 11 at K-13 in 1952. Tiger teeth were painted on F-86s of the 25th FIS's Tiger Flight. The F-86E-1, E-5, and E-6 had a v-shaped armored windscreen. The mud on the nose wheel provides an indication of the crude conditions found on all the airfields in Korea. (Joe Weber)

The F-86 nose gear assembly retracted to the rear while the wheel turned 90°. The forward gear door was attached to both fuselage and the nose gear strut. A hydraulic power steering unit was mounted on the rear of the strut. (Author)

Nose Gear and Well

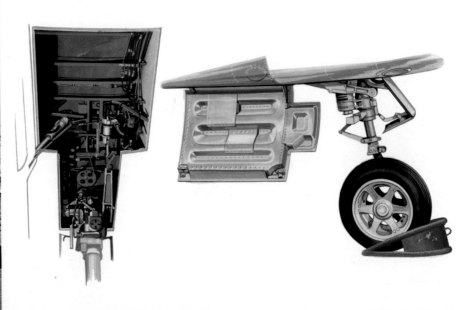

(Above) A camouflaged F-86A sits on the K-13 ramp during the summer of 1951. The natural metal Sabres were easily visible during daylight, however, camouflage netting was draped over the aircraft to hide them from the prying eye of 'Bedcheck Charlie' — a North Korean or Chinese Po-2 biplane that often visited the base at night. This F-86A has an unpainted brown fiberglass nose intake. (Irv Clark)

(Below) F-86s on the alert ramp at Johnson AB, Japan display the many different markings found on the 4th FIG's Sabres during 1951. All four aircraft have the fiberglass intakes, although only one intake remains brown. The two types of nose wheel are also evident — the early open six-spoked wheel and the later closed 12-spoked wheel. These aircraft are assigned to the 334th FIS and display either a yellow nose stripe or a 'winged star' marking. (Lon Walter)

(Above) This was not a captured F-86A, but a 'MiG' for the movie 'Sabre Jet,' a film starring Robert Stack. Several aircraft from the Fighter School at Nellis AFB, Nevada were painted in 'MiG' markings and used to combat other Sabres for the flying scenes in the 1953 movie about the air war in Korea. (Dick Gilbert)

9

Most F-86s were equipped with the later Cleveland AN-W-6 12-fin cast nose wheel. The wheel mounted a six-ply, smooth tread, high pressure tire. The F-86F was equipped with a 14-ply tire. The interior of the nose wheel well was painted Interior Green (FS34151), while the doors were painted silver. (NAA)

The F-86 nose gear was equipped with a power steering unit located behind the strut and above the v-shaped scissor link. This is the nose gear assembly for the first XP-86 and has the landing gear and door interiors painted light gray to match the exterior. The wheel is equipped with a non-standard circumferential treaded tire. (NAA)

A pair of landing lights was recessed into the underside of the nose. These lights rotated down and forward for operation. This 12th FBS F-86F was hit by Communist flak on 10 June 1953. The flak damaged the gun camera and port landing light. (Ebe Ebersole)

A hydraulic ram closed the aft nose wheel well door. The wheel well of this XP-86 is painted light gray, however, production aircraft used Interior Green (FS34151). The natural metal plates on the aft wheel well door were strengtheners added to production F-86s. (NAA)

MARLENE/MARIAN/NANCY, an F-86F from the 39th FIS, wears a variation of the tail markings used by the 51st FIG. Four-inch black and white checks replaced the standard 12-inch (30.5 cm) black and silver checkerboard. The device around the intake area is a screen to keep out foreign objects during engine runup tests. This aircraft is an F-86F-1, which has had the '6-3 hard wing' kit retrofitted to the existing wing. (Author)

SUNNY, an F-86E-6 from the 25th FIS, 51st FIW at Suwon, is surrounded by some of the equipment needed to operate the F-86 in Korea during the winter of 1952. The type C-6 auxiliary power cart was used to power up the aircraft, while the gasoline-powered heater fed hot air into the intake to warm the engine oil. Temperatures in Korea often fell to -20° Fahrenheit or lower during the winter. (USAF)

(Above) Col Ben Preston of the 4th FIG flew LIL' PUNKIN' while stationed in Korea. The ammunition bay access door is open and served as a step to the cockpit. The small rectangular door under the vertical black stripe covered an additional step used to enter the cockpit. The circular door below and behind the gun ports provided access to the nose gear trunnion pin. (Marty Isham)

(Below) PUDDY TAT, a 12th FBS F-86F, undergoes an engine change at K-55 during the spring of 1953. The entire aft fuselage could be removed for engine access. Other open panels provide access to the radio and engine accessory compartments. This aircraft was one of the first F-86F-30s in Korea and was equipped with the reinforced wing with leading edge slats. (Dick Kempthorne)

(Above) "DE" JOISEY BOUNCE/JUDY ANN was an F-86E assigned to the 25th FIS at K-13 in 1952. The two small buttons in front of the vertical black stripe are the external canopy operating switches. A folding handhold, just visible above the two Ns in 'ANN', was incorporated into the upper portion of the gun bay door. (Herb Goldstein)

Little Rita was flown by Lt Dick Geiger of the 16th FIS in 1953. *Rita* was one of the early F-86Fs modified with the '6-3 hard wing.' The leading edge fillet plate, which extends over the ammunition door, sits atop the wing. The landing gear doors 'bleed down' after hydraulic pressure was reduced following engine shutdown. Once the engine was powered up, the doors immediately returned to the closed position. (Dick Geiger)

Among the most colorful Sabres were those flown by the RCAF 'Golden Hawks' aerobatic team. The team used Sabre Mark 5s and 6s with both the '6-3 hard wing' and leading edge slats. The 'Golden Hawks' performed displays from 1959 until 1964. This aircraft (23651) was displayed at Andrews AFB, Maryland in May of 1962. (Robert Mikesh)

Five F-86As from the 336th FIS are parked on the PSP ramp at Suwon AB in June of 1951. These aircraft wore black and white identification bands for quick identification in combat. The identification bands were necessary due to the resemblance of the F-86 to the MiG-15. All five aircraft have their slats in the down position — a normal condition when the F-86 was at rest. (USAF)

PEACEMAKER, an F-86E-6 assigned to the 334th FIS, exhibits the later markings of the 4th FIW in Korea. Black and yellow wing and fuselage bands were used by the Far East Air Force (FEAF) as identification markings. The 4th FIW also used these colors on the tail. PEACEMAKER was one of the 60 F-86E-6s built by Canadair for the US Air Force. (Curt Francom)

(Above) An F-86A scrambles from Suwon in August of 1951. The long plume of black smoke was a characteristic of early General Electric J47 engines. The later J47-27 engine used in the F-86F was more efficient than the -7 and -13 engines found in the earlier A and E models and left a reduced smoke trail. The aircraft carries 120 gallon (454.2 liter) underwing combat drop tanks to extend their range. (USAF)

(Below) This F-86F was the personal aircraft of BGen Roberts, the CO of the USAF Fighter School at Nellis AFB, Nevada. The school trained new F-86 pilots. Roberts' aircraft has six colored bands on the fuselage and drop tanks — one for each squadron assigned to the school. This aircraft is carrying the later style 200 gallon (757 liter) drop tanks with stabilizing vertical fins. F-86s were equipped with a hydraulically operated speed brake on both sides of the aft fuselage. (Merle Olmsted)

Major 'Hap' Harris sits in the cockpit of his F-86E, WYOMING THUNDER, while assigned to the 25th FIS during 1952. The Sabre had two gun bays — one on each side of the cockpit — with each bay mounting three .50 caliber (12.7 ᴍᴍ) M3 machine guns. Each weapon was fed by a 300-round capacity ammunition box mounted beneath the cockpit. The M3 machine gun had a cyclic rate of fire of over 1200 rounds per minute. (Don Porter)

The gun bay was painted silver, while most of the interior fittings — including the ammunition feed chutes — were natural metal. Each gun had its own feed chute that led up from the ammunition boxes in the bottom of the fuselage. Expended shell casings were dropped back into a fuselage bin and collected after landing. (Author)

Gun Doors

Browning M3 .50 Caliber Machine Gun

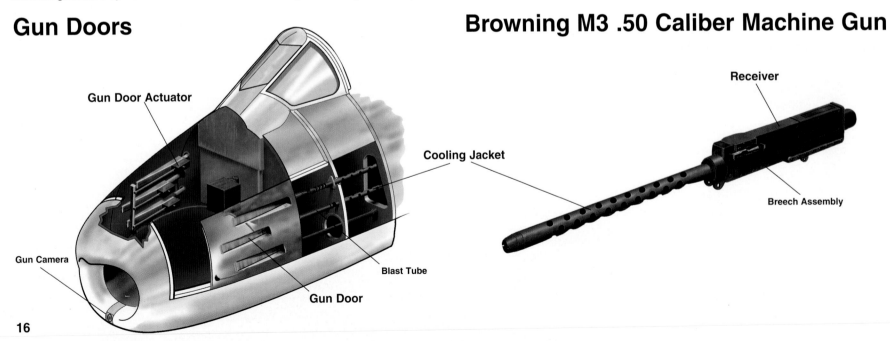

Gun Door Actuator

Gun Camera

Cooling Jacket

Blast Tube

Gun Door

Receiver

Breech Assembly

Gun Bay (Starboard Side)

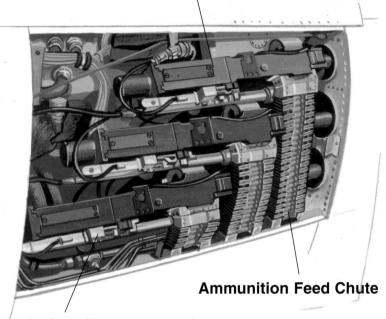

Browning .50 caliber M3 Machine Gun

Ammunition Feed Chute

Electric Gun Charger

Ammunition Bay (Starboard Side)

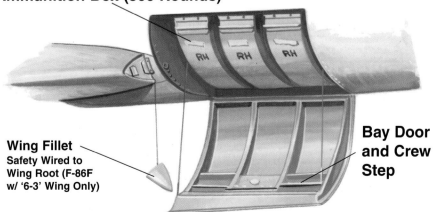

Ammunition Box (300 Rounds)

RH RH RH

Wing Fillet
Safety Wired to
Wing Root (F-86F
w/ '6-3' Wing Only)

Bay Door and Crew Step

The breech cover on the No. 1 gun of this 51st Wing F-86E is open. The guns and their feed chutes were staggered fore-and-aft to match the order of the ammunition boxes mounted beneath the cockpit. The M3 machine guns were charged on the ground prior to a mission. (Hank Buttlemann)

The guns were angled to improve ammunition feed and prevent jamming. All six guns were boresighted to converge at 1200 feet (365.8 M). SISSY was an F-86F assigned to the 12th FBS in 1953. (John Dawson)

17

(Above) Each M3 machine gun was equipped with an electric gun charger — the silver colored mechanism mounted on the side of the gun breech. The linked .50 caliber ammunition belts came up from the ammunition containers through aluminum feed chutes and into the breech. This is the starboard gun bay of an F-86A. (Author)

(Left) Col Harrison Thyng, commander of the 33rd FIW, Otis AFB, Massachusetts, climbs into his F-86A in the summer of 1951. The normal ingress procedure was to grab the folding handle incorporated into the gun bay door, step onto the ammunition bay door, and then put the left foot into the retractable door just under the black stripe. Col Thyng scored five victories while flying Spitfires in World War Two and added five MiGs to his total in 1952 while commanding the 4th FIW in Korea. (USAF)

(Below) A/2C David Dawson, an armorer with the 44th FBS, replaces the lower M3 gun at Clark AB, Philippines on 26 July 1954. The 69-pound (31.3 KG) guns were man-handled into the gun bay, then pushed forward into position before being locked in place. The ammunition boxes, each holding up to 300 rounds, were installed in the open bay under the guns. The ammunition boxes could be loaded while on the aircraft, although this procedure was rare. (USAF)

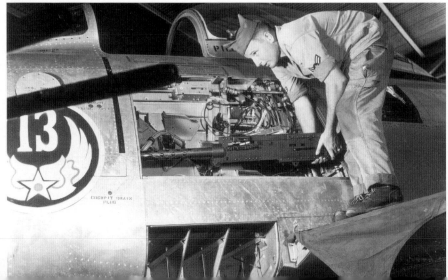

(Above) A 12th FBS armorer loads .50 caliber rounds into the ammunition boxes of an F-86F on Formosa on 14 February 1955. This aircraft is one of the factory-built F-86Fs with the '6-3 hard wing'. F-86s equipped with this wing had bulged ammunition doors and a removable fillet on the wing leading edge. (USAF)

(Right) Capt Lonnie Moore flew *Billie*/Margie , an F-86F, while assigned to the 335th FIS at Kimpo in 1953. The large triangular piece sitting on the wing is the fillet panel that extended the '6-3' wing leading edge over the gun bay door. The leading edge 'kits' supplied by North American in late 1952 had a removable fillet to allow access to the ammunition compartment. (USAF)

(Below) 4th FIG armorers wipe down the gun panel of an OPERATION STOVEPIPE F-86A at Suwon during the fall of 1951. The gun panels were wiped with oil prior to a mission. The oil trapped residue when the guns were fired. Crew chiefs used the oily residue as a quick indication that the weapons had been fired. The panels were cleaned immediately after a mission. (Arthur O'Neil)

19

4th FIW armorers and crew chiefs work on the port side guns of *VIRGINIA BELLE*, an F-86E assigned to the 335th FIS. The ammunition feeds are filled and the armorer will lay the ammunition into the breech mechanism. The guns were not charged until immediately prior to a mission. (Author)

Lt Jim Thompson flew THE HUFF, an F-86F, while assigned to the 39th FIS in Korea. The dragon marking was applied after Lt Thompson shot down a Chinese MiG-15 that had a large dragon painted on its side. It was necessary to remove the wing root portion of the leading edge fillet in order to open the ammunition bay door. Some aircraft had the fillet safety wired to the airframe to prevent its loss during maintenance. (D.N. Drew)

The radio servicing panel has been removed on this 336th FIS F-86F. The radio could be completely replaced in about five minutes. The yellow panel above the radio bay is the emergency canopy release. An Automatic Direction Finding (ADF) antenna dome — under the rear of the canopy — was mounted on the sliding canopy frame. (Tom Clarke)

Crew chiefs install a '6-3 hard wing kit' on an F-86F-30 assigned to the 67th FBS, 18th FBW at Osan in May of 1953. The complete leading edge and slat mechanism was removed and replaced with one of the factory-designed 'kits.' The '6-3 hard wing' could be installed on any F-86F as well as some F-86Es. North American supplied at least 150 kits to the combat units in Korea. (Harvey Brown)

(Above) Lt Sam Johnson flew this F-86F, SHIRLEY'S TEXAS TORNADO, while assigned to the 16th FIS at K-13 in 1953. Lt Johnson is now a US Congressman. The open door just in front of the speed brakes provided access to the engine and flight control connections. The flight controls were disconnected when the aft fuselage was removed for maintenance. (Sam Johnson)

(Below) This F-86F-40 was assigned to the Republic of Korea Air Force's 10th FW at Osan AB on 28 August 1975. ROKAF Sabres were ex-USAF aircraft equipped with 12-inch (30 CM) extended wingtips and provisions for AIM-9 Sidewinder air-to-air missiles. ROKAF F-86s were camouflaged in USAF Southeast Asia colors of Dark Green (FS34079), Olive Green (FS34102), and Tan (FS30219), with Light Gray (FS36622) undersides. (Stephen Miller)

21

The third highest scoring ace in Korea, Capt Manuel J. 'Pete' Fernandez, prepares to board his second F-86E (51-2857). The stars under the canopy represent the pilot's total score. The upside down stars under the ground crew block indicate kills achieved while in service with the current crew chief. This method of indicating kills was unique to the 4th FIW. All of 'Pete' Fernandez's victories were achieved while flying F-86Es with the 334th FIS. (Don Miller)

An armorer feeds a belt of .50 caliber rounds into the ammunition bay on a 21st FBW F-86F at Chambley AB, France in 1955. The F-86F-35 was the only 'F' variant capable of delivering a nuclear weapon and used a Low Altitude Bombing System (LABS) computer to 'toss' the weapon at the target. A 750 LB (340.2 KG) M117 bomb is on the bomb cart in the foreground. (NAA)

(Above) Crew chiefs stand next to Irva Jean just after boresighting the guns of this 335th Fighter Day Squadron (FDS) F-86F in 1956. The M3 machine guns were boresighted to converge at 1200 feet (365.8 м). The aircraft was raised on jacks to reduce vibration in order to achieve more accurate sighting. Fighter day squadrons were tasked with the air superiority mission. (USAF)

(Right) An armorer removes live ammunition from Major Bill Whisner's F-86E, Elenore E/CHRISTINE. His assistant removes spent ammunition and links from the lower bay. Spent ammunition was accessed through a door in the nose wheel well. Maj Whisner scored two MiG kills with the 4th FIW and 3.5 MiG kills with the 51st FIW. These victories were in addition to his 15.5 kills scored in World War Two while serving with the 352nd FG. (USAF)

23

(Above) An F-86A assigned to the 94th FS at March Field in 1949 carries 206.5 gallon (781.7 liter) underwing ferry tanks. The circular design of the ferry tanks caused buffeting at high Mach numbers, restricting the Sabre's maximum speed to .8 Mach. (H.G. Martin)

(Below) An F-86F-30 from the 67th FBS carries a full load of fuel tanks prior to a mission from Osan during 1953. The F-30 featured a strengthened wing with four underwing hard points. The inboard hard points carry 120 gallon (454.2 liter) Misawa drop tanks, while 120 gallon combat tanks are mounted on the outboard hard points. (James Sullivan)

(Above) An F-86E of the 25th FIS rests on jacks in the gun harmonizing pits at Suwon AB, Korea. The Sabre carries a pair of 120 gallon (454.2 liter) combat tanks manufactured in Misawa, Japan for use in Korea. Misawa tanks had some unfavorable separation characteristics and were often painted Olive Drab to remind the pilot to take the appropriate action if they had to be dropped. (Bob Brackett)

(Above) Faster aircraft and more powerful engines required changes in drop tank design. This F-86F has a pair of 200 gallon (757 liter) combat drop tanks mounted under the wings. The sway-backed appearance of the tanks was designed to improve separation at high air speeds. Later, small vertical fins were added to the rear of the tank for additional stability at higher speeds. This F-86F was assigned to the 50th Fighter Bomber Wing (FBW) at Hahn AB, Germany in 1954. (Maj. Emmett Hatch)

(Above Left) Drop tanks were in such demand in Korea that they were stored by the hundreds. It was not unusual for a Sabre wing to go through over 100 drop tanks in a single day if the MiGs were aggressive. One hundred twenty gallon (454.2 liter) combat tanks are in the foreground, while 120 gallon Misawa tanks are stored behind them. The tanks were built up and stored complete with the anti-sway brace attached to the tank. (Bill Grover)

Drop Tanks

120 Gallon Combat Tank

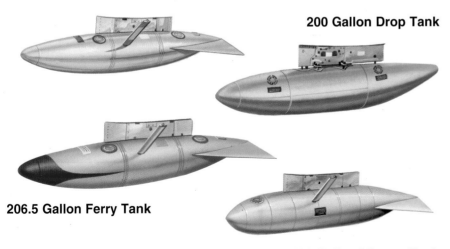

200 Gallon Drop Tank

206.5 Gallon Ferry Tank

120 Gallon Misawa Tank

(Below) HOT STUFF was an F-86F-30 serving with the Philippine Air Force. This Sabre carries a pair of Mitsubishi-designed 200 gallon (757 liter) drop tanks, which lacked stabilizing fins. HOT STUFF is a rare bird — F-86s not in service with American units seldom carried nose art or personal markings. Philippine F-86Fs were painted overall silver to retard corrosion. (via David Menard)

25

(Below) Flight tests revealed problems during combat maneuvers while carrying 206.5 gallon (781.7 liter) ferry tanks. North American engineers designed the 120 gallon (454.2 liter) 'combat drop tank' as a result of these tests. This tank could be flown to speeds at or near Mach One. Combat tanks also had small braces installed on the outboard side to improve lateral stability. (USAFM)

(Above) This F-86A assigned to the Fighter School at Las Vegas AFB (later Nellis AFB), Nevada carries a pair of 206.5 gallon (781.6 liter) ferry tanks provided with every Sabre delivered during 1949. Additionally, the tanks were braced on both sides to prevent the tank from swaying laterally while in flight. This early F-86A-5 has both gun doors and the fiberglass intake without a small radome in the upper lip. Las Vegas AFB was renamed Nellis AFB in 1950. (USAF)

(Below) The 120 gallon (454.2 liter) combat drop tanks were not circular in shape; they had flattened upper surfaces to reduce the effect of shock waves created between the top of the tank and the wing. The combat tanks had small stabilizing fins installed which had a 17° cathedral (pronounced cat-he-dral — another term for anhedral). (USAFM)

(Above) The Old Man, an F-86F-30 assigned to the 8th FBG, is posed with the variety of ordnance carried by this aircraft. From right: 500 LB (226.8 KG) M43 General Purpose bomb, 750 LB (340.2 KG) M117 GP bomb, and 1000 LB (453.6 KG) M64A1 GP bomb with conical fin section. Belts of .50 caliber (12.7 MM) machine gun ammunition are displayed in front of the aircraft. The maximum ammunition load was 1800 rounds. This Sabre was the personal aircraft of Col Walter Benz, commander of the 8th FBG. (NAA)

(Right) The drop tank situation in Korea became critical when the second F-86 wing became operational in 1952. Far East Air Force Air Material Command (FEAMCOM) authorized hundreds of Misawa tanks — originally built for the Lockheed F-80 Shooting Star — to be modified for use by F-86 Sabres. The conversion involved the installation of 17° cathedral fins and changing the carriage lugs to fit the F-86 drop tank pylon. (USAF)

Rocket Launcher

Front Pylon

Rear Pylon

(Above) The 4th FIG pulled out of Korea ahead of the Chinese advance in January of 1951. Although a fighter-interceptor unit, the unit began flying fighter-bomber sorties from Taegu after returning to Korea in February. This F-86A, belonging to Col Glenn Eagleston, has a 5-inch (12.7 CM) High Velocity Aircraft Rocket (HVAR) fitted inboard of the drop tank. The F-86A could only carry two rockets when drop tanks were carried. (Wm. J. O'Donnell)

(Below) BEVKENEVE, an F-86F assigned to No. 2 Squadron, South African Air Force, carries the standard fighter-bomber ordnance load in Korea — two 120 gallon (454.2 liter) drop tanks and two 1000 LB (453.6 KG) bombs. No. 2 Squadron was assigned to the 18th FBG at Osan AB and converted from F-51D Mustangs to F-86Fs during the first half of 1953. (Paul Barranger)

Bomb Rack and Pylon

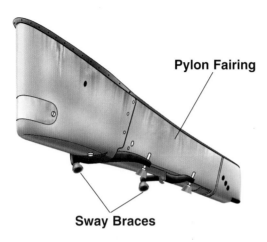

Pylon Fairing

Sway Braces

(Below) A 67TH FBS F-86F-30 stands five-minute alert at Osan AB in 1953. This Sabre is fitted with two 1000 LB bombs and two 120 gallon (454.2 liter) combat drop tanks. An additional hard point was placed under each wing of this F-30. A five-inch (12.7 CM) high flow fence was added to the wing when the '6-3 hard wing' leading edge was installed. (James Sullivan)

(Above) A 67th FBS pilot and his crew chief check the nose wheel steering on an F-86F at Osan during the summer of 1953. An M64A1 1000 LB (453.6 KG) bomb is fitted with the new style conical fin section. This type of fin structure began appearing in Korea during early 1953. (USAF)

(Above) Armorers assigned to No. 2 Squadron, SAAF screw fuses into the nose and tail of an M64 1000 LB (453.6 KG) bomb at Osan during May of 1953. A wire was connected to the safety pins once the fuses were in place. The pins kept the bombs from 'arming' until they were dropped. (SAAF)

(Left) Weapons personnel unload an M64 1000 LB bomb from a bomb truck at Suwon on 18 June 1953, while armorers guide another bomb under the wing of The Georgia Peach, an 8th FBG F-86F. The truck delivered the bombs to the cart, which was set up to mate the bomb to the underside of the wing at the exact angle required for installation. (USAF)

(Below) Armorers from the 8th FBG guide one of the new style M64A1 1000 LB bombs to the inboard wing pylon of an F-86F fighter bomber in July of 1953. The 8th FBG at Suwon converted from Lockheed F-80Cs to F-86F fighter-bombers in May of 1953, becoming the fourth F-86 wing in Korea. (Author)

A bomb delivery truck brings 1000 LB (453.6 KG) M64 bombs to the armorers of GLOW WORM, an F-86F assigned to No. 2 Squadron, SAAF. No. 2 Squadron F-86Fs were drawn from USAF stocks and 'loaned' to the South African squadron until the late summer of 1953 when the unit rotated home. (SAAF)

A 67th FBS pilot uses a wooden ladder — borrowed from an F-84G — to board his F-86F in the summer of 1953. 18th FBG Sabres flew close support and long range strikes against targets deep in 'MiG Alley.' The first flights of the new Sabre squadrons were integrated into the air superiority strikes flown by the 4th and 51st FIGs. (NAA)

(Above) A 'bombed up' F-86F from the 35th FBS rests in a revetment at Suwon during the summer of 1953. This Sabre carries a pair of M43 500 LB (226.8 KG) bombs and two 120 gallon (454.2 liter) Misawa drop tanks. The employment of 500 LB bombs usually indicated a strike against a target deep in 'MiG Alley' at the extreme end of the F-86F's range — closer targets usually warranted 1000 LB bombs. The 8th FBG converted to slat-wing F-86F-30s in May of 1953. (Paul Barranger)

(Below) An F-86F-35, assigned to the 388th FBW at Etain AB, France in 1955, carries four drop tanks under its wings. A pair of 200 gallon (757 liter) tanks are mounted on the outboard pylons, and two 120 gallon (454.2 liter) tanks are fitted to the inboard pylons. The 388th deployed to Etain in November of 1954 as part of a nuclear strike force. The F-86F-35 was the only nuclear capable variant of the F-86F series. (M. Van Gerpen)

(Above) *Miss Tena* was the personal F-86F of Col Woodrow Wilmot, the 8th FBG commander at Suwon in 1954. Col Wilmot's Sabre carries the multiple colored stripes on the nose and tail signifying a group or wing commander's aircraft. All F-86Fs in Korea had been converted to the '6-3 hard wing' by 1954. A 100 LB (45 KG) practice bomb is mounted under the port wing. (Jim Carter)

(Above) Armorers stack M64A1 1000 LB (453.6 KG) bombs behind THE STINGER, an F-86F fighter bomber from the 12th FBS at Osan in 1953. Nearest to the camera are M43 500 LB (226.8 KG) bombs fitted with the new conical fins. These bombs sit on wooden racks to have the fins and proper lug spacing attached by armorers. (Bill Grover)

BLACK DICK and IMP VIII, a pair of No. 2 Squadron F-86Fs, leave Osan-ni under a stormy sky carrying 1000 LB (453.6 KG) bombs and drop tanks. No. 2 Squadron returned their Sabres to the USAF and rotated home to South Africa on 29 September 1953. (NAA)

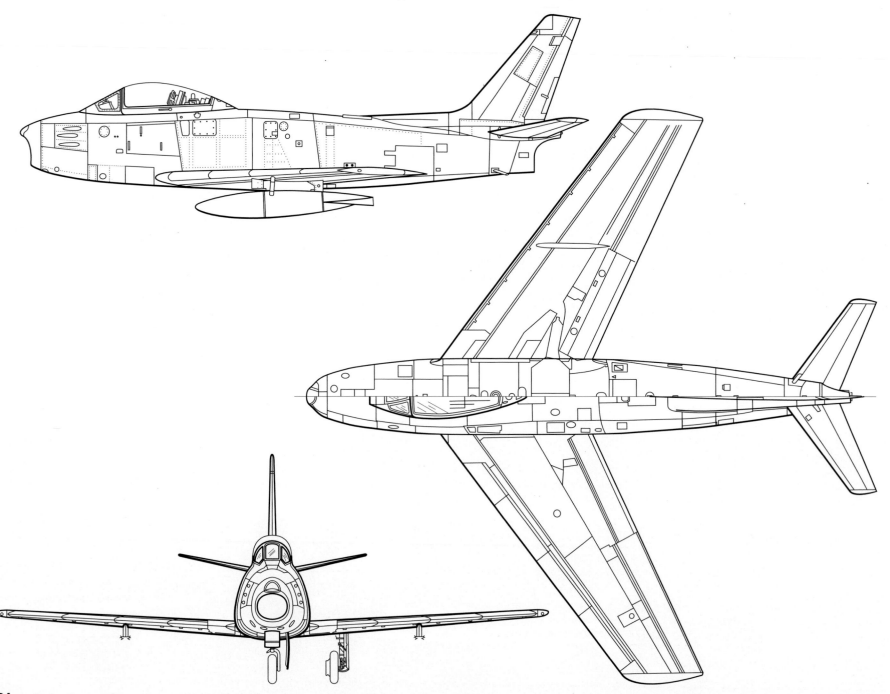

F-86A Port Profile

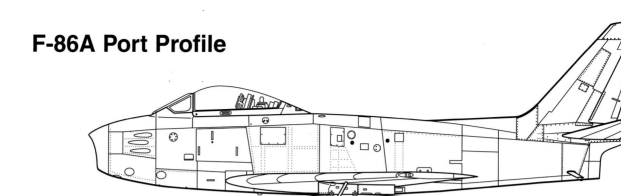

F-86E Specifications

Powerplant: J47-GE-13 w/5200 LBS of thrust @ 7950 RPM
Dimensions
Wing span...............37.12 feet (11.31 M)
Length.....................37.54 feet (11.44 M)
Height....................14.74 feet (4.49 M)
Track........................8.3 feet (2.53 M)
Weights (LBS)
Fuel (JP-4 at 6.6 LBS/gallon)
Internal...................435 gallons (1646.6 L), 2871 LBS (1302.3
                          KG)
Ammunition...........1800 rounds, 480 LBS (217.7 KG)
Combat weight......14,255 LBS (6466 KG)
Landing weight......12,557 LBS (5695.8 KG)

Performance
Take-off stall speed............123 MPH (198 KM)
Ferry range.........................1022 miles (1644.7 KM)
Combat radius....................321 miles (516.6 KM) @ 537 MPH
                                 (864.2 KMH)
Total mission time...............1.57 hours
Maximum speed...................679 MPH (1092.7 KMH) at sea
                                level, 601 MPH (967.2 KMH) at
                                35,000 feet (10,668 M)
Maximum climb...................7250 feet (2209.8 M)/minute at
                                sea level
Service ceiling....................47,200 feet (14,386.5 M)

RF-86A Port Profile

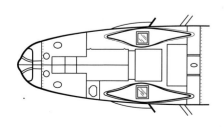
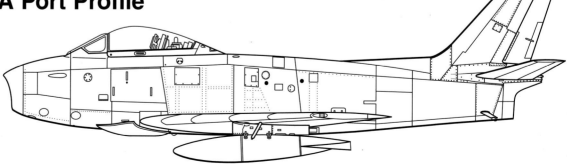

Col Harrison R. Thyng sits in the cockpit of his F-86E, "Pretty Mary & The Js", at Kimpo in 1952. The canopy slide track is located on top of the fuselage. Col Thyng's type P3 helmet sits on top of the v-shaped windscreen found on F-86As and early F-86Es. His helmet bears the colors of the 4th FIW's three squadrons — the 334th FIS, the 335th FIS, and the 336th FIS. Col Thyng commanded the 4th FIW in 1952. (Harrison Thyng)

The instrument panel and right console of a Canadair Sabre Mk. 6 featured a different instrument cluster than USAF Sabres. The basic cockpit color was changed from Interior Green (FS34151) with a black instrument panel to Interior Gray (FS36231) on all Sabres in 1953. (Phillipe Joris)

The F-86F-30's gyro compass was mounted in the center of the black instrument panel. Red buttons on the control stick are for weapons release (top) and radar target selector switch (bottom). The F-86F was equipped with the type A-4 gun sight assembly. (Dick Kempthorne)

The type A-4 gun sight could be used on F-86Es and Fs, replacing the A-1CM sight fitted to F-86As and early Es. The dial under the sight glass was set at the opposing aircraft's wingspan. Once the gun sight computer determined that the aircraft was within the optimum range for a 'kill,' the sight reticle brightened and the pilot pulled the trigger. (Dick Kempthorne)

F-86F Cockpit Layout (Typical)

Type A-4 Gunsight

Instrument Panel

Port Console

Starboard Console

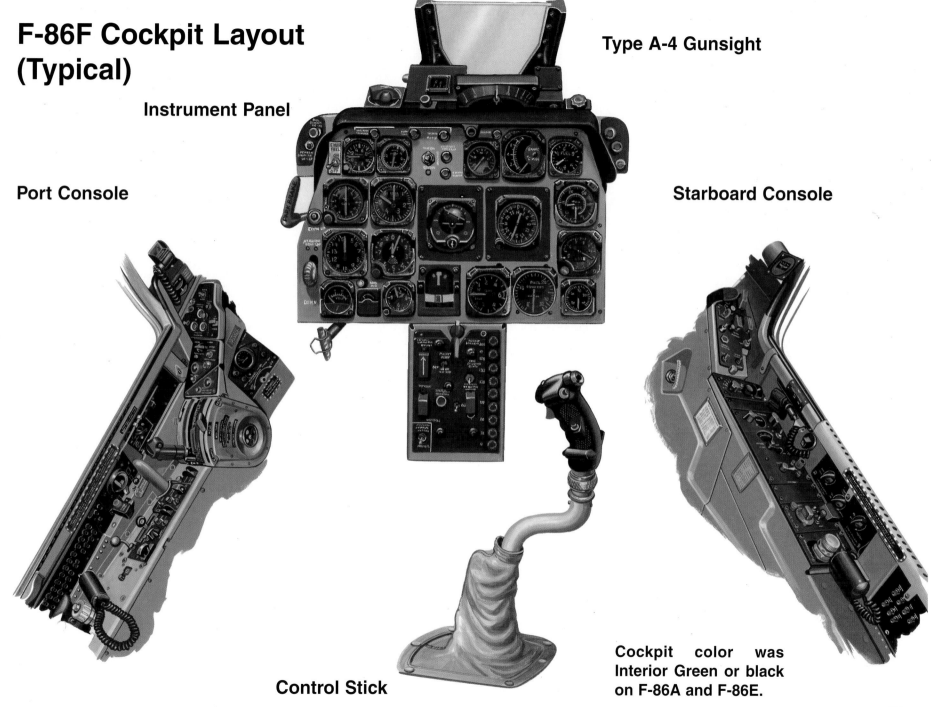

Control Stick

Cockpit color was Interior Green or black on F-86A and F-86E.

The Sperry Mk 18 gun sight which equipped early F-86As was the same unit found on North American's P-51D Mustang. Mk.18 sights used on the Sabre, however, had a different mount and were tied into the Sabre's AN/APG-5C ranging radar assembly. (NAA)

The type A-1CM gun sight replaced the Mk 18 sight on later F-86As and F-86Es. Problems with the A-1CM sight system led to its replacement by the type A-4 unit, which was easier to maintain. (USAF)

A-1CM Gunsight (F-86A, E, F-1, and F-5)

A-4 Gunsight (F-86F-10 and Later)

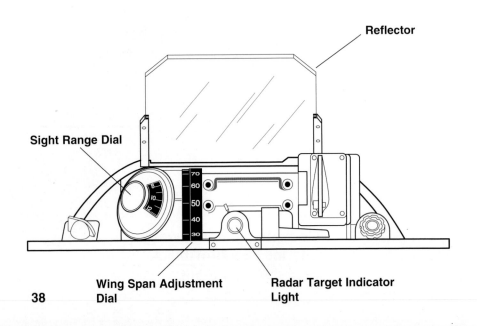

Reflector

Sight Range Dial

Wing Span Adjustment Dial

Radar Target Indicator Light

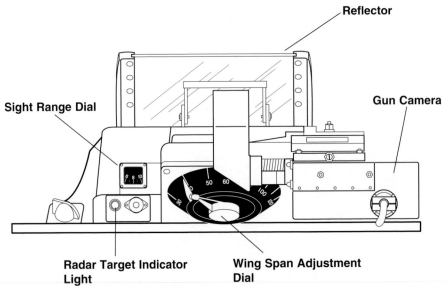

Reflector

Sight Range Dial

Gun Camera

Radar Target Indicator Light

Wing Span Adjustment Dial

The F-86 cockpit was complicated compared to piston-engined fighters such as the P-51. The ejection seat and armored wall separated the pilot from the radio direction finder (RDF) loop antenna, which was mounted on the canopy brace. The cockpit pressure regulator is the circular item mounted on the rear wall of the sliding canopy. The rear view mirror was mounted directly to the inside of the canopy. (NAA)

Angle of attack lines were placed inside the canopy of the F-86F fighter-bomber. These lines were printed on large pieces of film and could be easily removed if necessary. Sabre pilots used these lines to assist in lining up the correct dive angle for their attack runs. The RDF antenna dome is mounted on the back side of the main canopy frame brace. The rear of the mirror mount was painted flat black. (NAA)

The top of the ejector seat and rocket catapult mechanism is located under the sliding canopy. The catapult mechanism and the canopy extractor rocket are connected by a line. The small handle near the headrest was used for adjusting the height of the pilot's seat. (NAA)

The armament primary control panel was fitted to the left side of the F-86F-30 instrument panel. Both rudder pedals were embossed with the North American Aviation logo. The rudder trim switch was located on top of the control stick. The USAF began to phase out the use of Interior Green (FS34151) in 1953. Later cockpits were painted Interior Grey (FS36231). The instrument panels and consoles remained black. (NAA)

Ejection Seat

Chest Belts

The canopy extractor and slide mounts were located under the sliding portion of the canopy. The back wall of the rocket catapult was armor plate to protect both the pilot and the catapult. The small diameter piping along both sides of the canopy directed warm demisting air onto the canopy glass. (Author)

Canopy and Cockpit Rear Deck

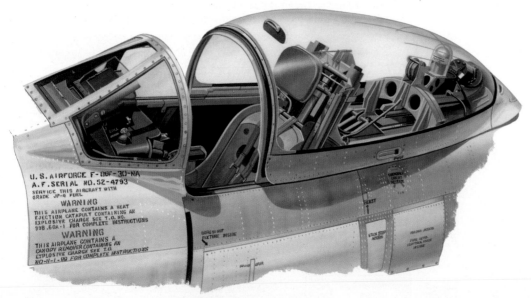

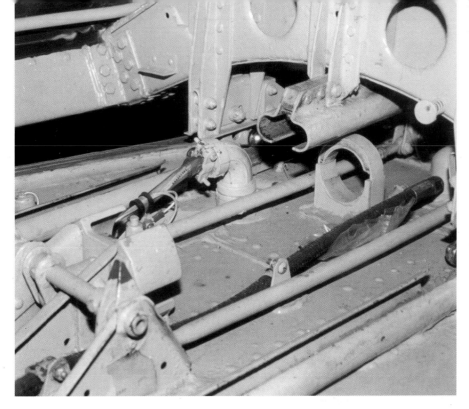

(Above) The canopy slide tracks were mounted on top of the rear decking. This area, originally Interior Green, was repainted Interior Gray. (Jim Walker)

(Above Right) The cockpit pressure regulator was mounted on the rear wall of the sliding canopy. The canopy frame was lined with sealing material to prevent pressure leaks. (Jim Walker)

(Right) Crew chiefs remove the sliding canopy from Major Jack Mass' 335th FIS F-86F to check on a canopy defrosting system problem. F-86s and MiGs fought at altitudes well over 45,000 feet (13,716 M). Rearward vision in the Sabre was often hampered by canopy frosting due to inadequate heating. The eight MiG kills painted on the right side of the aircraft indicate kills credited to the aircraft — not to the pilot. (Norm Green)

41

The first F-86E-10 from the North American factory displays the open leading edge slats and the new, flat windscreen used on both the late model F-86Es and all of the F models. The slats were aerodynamically actuated by air pressure at certain speeds and angles of attack. (NAA)

The underside of this battle-damaged F-86E displays the seven slat actuators, which guided the slat in and out at various speeds. A MiG-15's 23 MM cannon shell hit the wingtip of this 335th FIS Sabre in the summer of 1951. (NAA)

The first F-86E-10 displays the depth and angle of attack of its fully deployed leading edge slats. The slats deployed at speeds less than 205 MPH (330 KM), however, these could often be 'tricked' into extension by aerodynamic forces at high altitudes and speeds. These conditions created some unusual flight characteristics for the Sabre. (NAA)

Viewed from the F-86 cockpit, the port leading edge slat displays three of the seven actuators in their rectangular slots. The slat mechanisms were virtually identical throughout the Sabre variants — including the Canadair models. (Author)

Wing Development

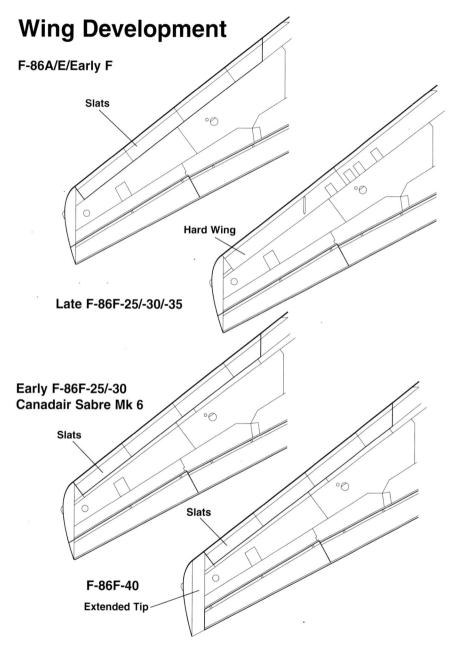

F-86A/E/Early F

Slats

Hard Wing

Late F-86F-25/-30/-35

Early F-86F-25/-30
Canadair Sabre Mk 6

Slats

Slats

F-86F-40

Extended Tip

The first '6-3 hard wing kits' began arriving in Korea in the fall of 1953. The shiny silver wing leading edge indicates these F-86Fs from the 39th FIS, 51st FIW, have had their kits installed. The entire leading edge of the wing was replaced when a '6-3 hard wing kit' was installed. (USAF)

Wing Slats

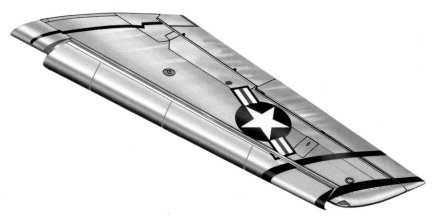

The wingtip light (red to port, green to starboard) on the F-86E and F was a small extruded type. This type replaced the larger wingtip light fairing on the F-86A. The aileron tip extended the wingtip on short span Sabre wings. This F-86E-6 was assigned to the 334th FIS at Kimpo in 1952. The pilot of this Sabre, Squadron Leader Eric Smith, was a Royal Canadian Air Force exchange officer. (S/L Eric Smith)

An F-86F fighter-bomber assigned to the 67th FBS sits runway alert at Osan-ni in 1953. This aircraft has the starter cart plugged in and the flaps already lowered. This F-86's dive brake door interiors were painted Interior Green (FS34151). Sabres had the bay interiors painted either Interior Green or silver. (James Sullivan)

Sabres were rarely found with the flaps in the down position, however, this F-86A assigned to the 4th FIG is an exception to the rule. The flaps were electrically operated and returned to 0° after landing. The Red stripe indicates a 'No Step' area, however, this was often ignored by mechanics when working on the engine accessories. (via David Menard)

(Above) Two 58th FBW F-86Fs fly over Korea in 1953. The five-inch (12.7 CM) high flow fence used on the '6-3 hard wing' is visible on the near aircraft's starboard wing. There is no reinforcement on the inboard side of the flow fence. (R.B. Ochs)

(Below) This F-86F-25 was assigned to the 53rd Fighter Day Squadron (FDS), 36th Fighter Day Wing (FDW) at Bitburg, Germany in 1954. The fences and tail band display the Wing colors, while the yellow fuselage stripes represent the 53rd FDS. A fighter day wing was another term for the air superiority mission for the 36th Wing. (Ford Smart)

(Above) Lt Earl Wisecarver stands by THE HUFF, a 39th FIS F-86F that was retrofitted with the '6-3 hard wing' at Suwon in 1953. The outboard edge of the fence has a small reinforcement plate at the base. The new leading edge displays a greater shine than the adjacent wing and fuselage surfaces. (Dean Abbott)

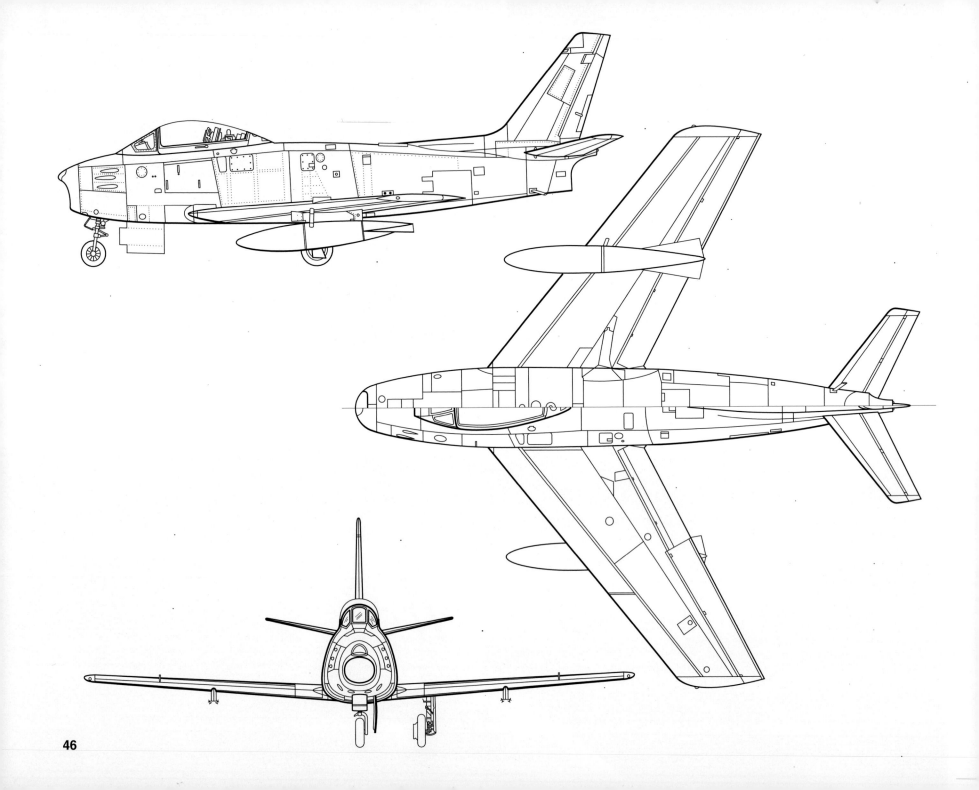

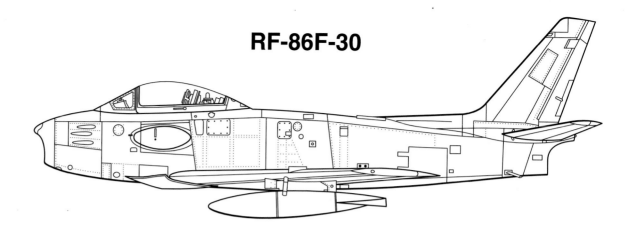

RF-86F-30

F-86F-30 Specifications
(w/ '6-3 hard wing')

Powerplant: J47-GE-27 with 5910 LBS of thrust at 7950 RPM
Dimensions:
Wing span....................37.12 feet (11.31 M)
Length.........................37.54 feet (11.44 M)
Height..........................14.74 feet (4.49 M)
Track............................8.3 feet (2.53 M)

Weights (lbs)
Fuel (JP-4 at 6.6 LBS (2.99 KG)/gallon)
Internal.........................437 gallons (1654.2 L), 2884.2 LBS
                                          (1308.3 KG)
Ammunition.................1800 rounds, 480 LBS (217.7 KG)
Combat weight............14,981 LBS (6795.4 KG)
Landing weight...........13,076 LBS (5931.3 KG)
Performance
Takeoff stall speed.....144 MPH (231.7 KMH)
Ferry range..................1615 miles (2599 KM)

Combat radius.............458 miles (737 KM) at 520 MPH (836.8
                                     KMH) cruise speed
Combat radius w/ two 1000 LBS (453.6 KG) bombs:
                                     316 miles (508.5 KM) at 486 MPH (782.1
                                     KMH) cruise speed.
Total mission time.......2.13 hours
Maximum speed..........695 MPH (1118.5 KMH) at sea level, 608
                                     MPH (978.4 KMH) at 35,000 feet (10,668 M)
Maximum climb rate...9300 feet (2834.6 M)/minute at sea level
Service ceiling.............48,000 feet (14,630.4 M)

Project 'Gunval' F-86F-2

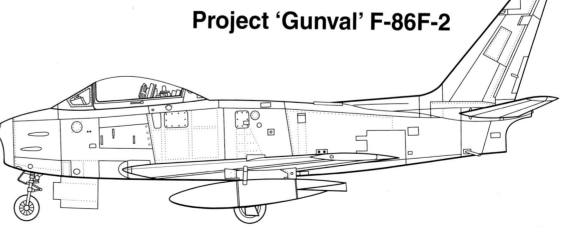

Main Landing Gear

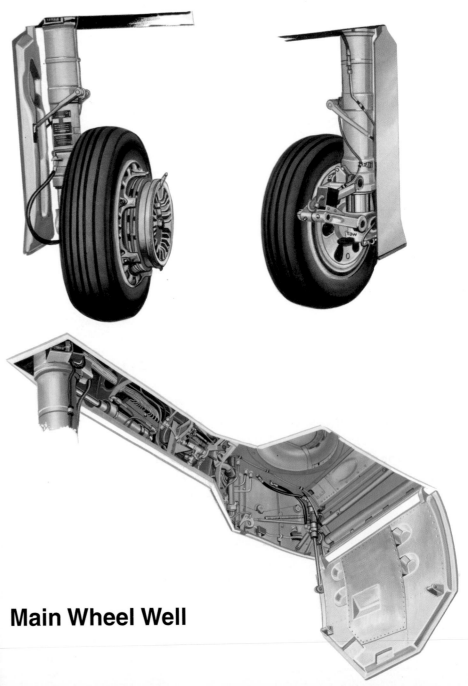

A green formation light was mounted on the right wingtip. The angled pitot tube lay parallel with the plane of the wing. This F-86F Sabre was assigned to the 4th FDW and stationed at Chitose AB, Japan in 1956. (Mike Fox)

There were many variations of Foreign Object Damage (FOD) screens used on Sabres. This 4th FIW F-86F employed a simple, heavy gauge wire assembly fitted over the intake to keep unwary mechanics from walking in front of the aircraft and being pulled into the intake duct. (Tom Clark)

Main Wheel Well

Speed Brake Bay

The C-6 auxiliary power cart was plugged into the electrical outlet just forward of the main fuel tank filler cap. Alert aircraft, such as Lt Dick Geiger's *Little Rita* of the 16th FIS, had the power cart plugged in at all times for fast engine starts. The wing leading edge fillet is resting on top of the wing near the fuselage. (Dick Geiger)

Joe Weber, a 25th FIS pilot, stands near the open speed brake bay of an F-86E at Suwon in 1953. Various speed brake actuators are located in this bay, which is painted Interior Green (FS34151). The lower arm of the speed brake was covered by a small door while the brake was closed. The upper arm did not have such a door. (Joe Weber)

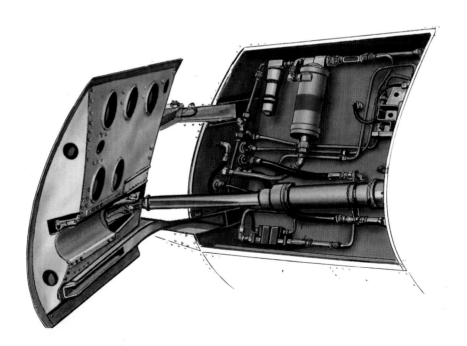

49

(Above) A1C George Tong fills the main fuel tank on a 199th FIS, Hawaii Air National Guard F-86E at Hickam AFB, Territory of Hawaii on 10 July 1956. The open door under the 'TH' is the access for the data case. Airman Tong is standing close to the wing flap, which is at full down position. (USAF)

(Left) A direct rear view of an F-86A shows the angle that the speed brakes open down into the air stream. The interior of the speed brake doors was painted Interior Green (FS 34151). The F-86A had a curved 'boat-tail' fairing with vertically mounted formation lights above the tailpipe. A fuel jettison pipe is mounted on the port side of the fuselage in front of the engine exhaust. (George McKay)

(Below) A Mitsubishi-built F-86F-40 from the 4th Fighter Squadron, Japanese Air Self Defense Force sits on the ramp at Komatsu AB, Japan in August of 1972. The F-40 differed from its USAF cousins by employing a slatted '6-3' wing, which was also extended 11 inches (27.9 CM) at each wingtip. This wing improved the Sabre's flying qualities. Additional engine cooling scoops have been added just forward of the speed brake. (Hideki Nagakubo)

(Above) The F-86A exhaust featured a segmented tail pipe. Small metal tabs — called 'mice' — were placed in the tailpipe opening to increase the exhaust temperature. This increased the aircraft's thrust and added two miles per hour (3.2 кмн) to the F-86's speed. 'Ratting the tailpipe' was a common occurrence on the combat Sabres in Korea, due to F-86 pilots seeking any performance advantage over the opposing MiG-15s. (Author)

(Right) North American Aviation mechanics make adjustments to the 'all-flying tail' on the first F-86E. The 'all-flying tail' had both the elevators and stabilizer hydraulically integrated to move together during flight. The controls were made irreversible at speeds at or above Mach One due to the incorporation of an artificial feel system into the 'all-flying tail'. These flight controls were installed on the F-86E and all subsequent Sabre models. (NAA)

(Below) A crew chief brushes snow off the fuselage of LICKITY SPLIT, a 51st FIG F-86E at K-13 during the winter of 1952. The opening at the bottom of the fuselage is an auxiliary engine cooling scoop. The airframe was covered by numerous servicing information stencils. (Fred Chapman)

Captain Simon Anderson makes a visual 'walk-around' of his F-86E-6 at Suwon in 1952. The aft fuselage of this aircraft has been replaced with a new section, which lacks the yellow FEAF ID band behind the engine break. Various sizes of the serial number digits indicate a replacement vertical tail. North American was very conscious of the lettering style and size when the aircraft left the factory. (Bob Brackett)

A 334th FIS F-86E rests on the Kimpo alert ramp in 1952 with everything ready to go — flaps down, power cart plugged in, and crew chief and armorer standing by under the wing. Five minute alert birds like this one had to be airborne minutes after being alerted since their job could be to protect a wounded comrade with MiGs on his tail. An F-86 usually took less than three minutes from engine start to be airborne. (Drury Callahan)

When mechanics take a Sabre apart, they really take it apart! This 4th FDW F-86F is about to undergo a complete Inspect and Repair As Necessary (IRAN) procedure. Virtually every compartment with a door was opened. The two large panels at mid-fuselage are for accessing the hydraulic reservoir (front) and the engine accessories bay — fuel pumps, oil pumps, and generators. (Mike Fox)

Squadron Leader Eric Smith, an RCAF exchange pilot on duty with the 334th FIS at Kimpo, flew this Canadair-built F-86E-6 in 1952. Spare drop tanks were often sitting in the revetment in case a mission aircraft required help, and the returning birds needed a quick turnaround. Sixty Canadair Sabre Mk 2s, redesignated F-86E-6 , were purchased by the USAF in 1952 for use in Korea. (S/L Eric Smith)

(Above) Col Donald Hall was the commander of the 4th FIW at Kimpo in late 1953. His F-86F, Dottie, carried markings not commonly found on 4th Wing aircraft. These included multi-color command bands around the fuselage and drop tanks and a 4th FIW emblem superimposed on the tail band. (Tom Clark)

(Below) Japanese Air Self Defense Force F-86F-40s were painted overall silver, and carried some colorful squadron markings. This aircraft was assigned to the 3rd Fighter Squadron at Misawa on 21 May 1975. This F-86 carries the 200 gallon (757 liter) unfinned drop tanks developed for the Sabre. Mitsubishi built 300 F-86F-40s for the JASDF. The F-40 wing was equipped with leading edge slats and a 12-inch (30.5 CM) extension at the wingtip. (Hideki Nagakubo)

(Above) This F-86F carries the early markings of the 18th FBW, worn immediately after the wing converted from the F-51D Mustang. The yellow nose and trim to the blue tail bands indicates an aircraft assigned to the 12th FBS. The lack of drop tanks usually indicated the aircraft had just returned from 'MiG Alley' and had sighted the enemy. Tanks were dropped before engaging the enemy to improve handling and performance during combat. The Sabres of the 18th FBW flew counter-air missions during their transition period. (Dave McLaren)

(Above) Sgt Dan Walker has his hand on the engine nose cover of the J47 engine that powered Capt Iven Kincheloe's F-86E. Disconnected electrical and hydraulic lines are left dangling in the aft fuselage section. These lines were disconnected from the forward fuselage when the tail section was removed for maintenance. Capt Kincheloe served in the 25th FIS. (Herb Goldstein via Robert F. Dorr)

(Left) Engine mechanics remove the J47-GE-27 engine from a 4th Fighter Wing F-86F at Kimpo during the summer of 1953. A large, portable crane was used to hoist the engine in and out of the aircraft. Kimpo had some permanent structures built for maintenance at this time, however, few facilities were completely enclosed against the Korean weather. (Don Miller)

(Below) The small panel and exit scoop located on top of the rear fuselage is the compressor overboard air bleed duct. This duct vented excess air from the compressor of the J47 engine. (Bill Neese)

(Above) The crew chief walks away from 1LT Hank Buttlemann's F-86E-6 after removing the aft section to service the engine. A special trailer was designed to support the rear fuselage of the Sabre. Small black stripes on the rear fuselage marked the exact position to place the supports. The inside of the engine bay was painted Interior Green (FS34151). (Hank Buttlemann)

(Right) During the cold Korean winter, hot air was pumped into the engine to warm the oil and hydraulic fluids prior to engine startup. The intake plug included a hole in the center to fit the hot air supply hose. Temperatures at Suwon and Kimpo often reached -20° Fahrenheit or lower.(Fred Chapman)

(Below) A crew chief from No. 2 Squadron, SAAF, removes the screws to access the Horizontal Stabilizer Control System. This system operated the F-86F's 'all-flying tail' assembly. Two other mechanics rewrap the tail pipe with a heat blanket prior to installation. Four hardened bolts held the aft fuselage to the forward fuselage. (NAA)

(Above) A rebuilt J47-GE-27 engine rests in the traveling dolly at Hazuke AB in June of 1951. The engine nose cone has been removed to access the engine generator and accessory drive section. Engines were rebuilt at Tachikawa (later at Tsuiki) and transported to Korea by large transport aircraft such as the Douglas C-124 Globemaster. (Budd Butcher)

(Below) A typical engine change in Korea took place on the open air ramp. Displayed at K-14 in 1952 are aircraft jack stands, flap sections (behind the J47 engine), additional tailpipes, drop tanks, and tool boxes of all sizes. An air compressor (at right) was used to tighten the many nuts and bolts, and was also used to paint the aircraft stripes. (Irv Clark)

(Above) Five 4th Fighter Wing mechanics make preliminary adjustments to a J47 engine prior to re-installation in an F-86A at Kimpo during the last half of 1951. The engine was mounted directly over the main fuel tank, located in the bottom of the engine bay. Two Australian Gloster Meteor Mk 8 fighters are parked in the background. (Irv Clark)

Thousands of miles from Korea, the maintenance facilities look the same. This F-86F-25 assigned to the 86th FBW underwent major engine maintenance on the open ramp at Landstuhl AB, Germany in March of 1954. The Cold War Warriors that stood 'Zulu Alert' with nuclear weapons at NATO bases throughout Western Europe were subjected to many of the same conditions that were found in Korea. The situation for these Sabres and their crews was just a little safer. (R.W. Blandin)

General Electric J47 Engine and Travel Dolly

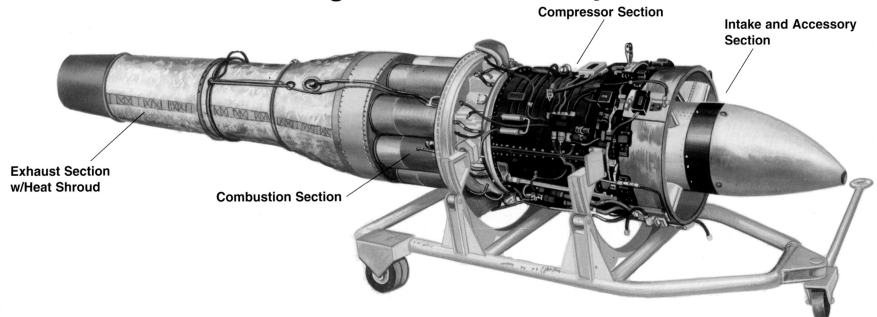

Compressor Section

Intake and Accessory Section

Exhaust Section w/Heat Shroud

Combustion Section

Several F-86A combat veterans from the 4th FIW were modified into reconnaissance aircraft at Tachikawa AB, Japan during the fall of 1951. These Sabres were equipped with two K-9 cameras mounted horizontally in the ammunition compartment. *Ruby Pearl*, a 15th TRS RF-86A, featured the bulged area that covered the camera bay. (George McKay)

KATHY was one of nine F-86As modified to RF-86A standards under Project ASHTRAY. Some of the ASHTRAY aircraft retained the upper pair of .50 caliber machine guns. Use of the guns was frowned upon since weapons firing shook the camera mounts and resulted in blurred photographs. RF-86As wore identical paint schemes to the 4th FIW fighter aircraft based across the field at Kimpo. (Bill Coffey)

Three F-86Fs were modified for the reconnaissance mission in 1953 under Project HAYMAKER. RF-86Fs were equipped with the same camera mount as those found on the ASHTRAY aircraft — a pair of horizontally mounted K-9 cameras in place of the ammunition bays. These aircraft, based on the F-86F-30 airframe, had the '6-3 hard wing' added when kits became available. (R.C. Beitel)

An unknown number of F-86F aircraft were modified on the North American Aviation production line into RF-86F reconnaissance aircraft. These Sabres were delivered to USAF and Republic of Korea squadrons after the end of the Korean War. The factory-built aircraft had vertically mounted cameras that required a large bulge in the (former) gun bay door to cover the magazine. This camouflaged RF-86F served with the ROKAF 10th Fighter Wing during the 1980s. (via Jim Sullivan)

(Above) Project GUNVAL was a North American Aviation program to increase F-86 firepower. Four F-86E-10 and six F-86F-1 airframes were pulled from the production line in 1952 and modified with four T-160 20 MM cannons in place of the six .50 caliber machine guns. The ten modified aircraft were redesignated the F-86F-2. (NAA)

(Below) Four GUNVAL F-86F-2s are parked on the 335th FIS ramp at Kimpo in early 1953. These tests lasted from January to May of 1953 with mixed results. GUNVAL pilots shot down 6.5 MiGs, however, cannon system problems kept the results low. The 20 MM T-160 cannon was later standardized as the M39 and used on the F-86H, F-100 Super Sabre, and F-101 Voodoo. Lt Col George Jones achieved 'ace' status in FU-867 directly below. (Paul Peterson)

(Above) Armorers from the GUNVAL test team work on one of the T-160 cannons at Kimpo in the spring of 1953. GUNVAL F-86F-2s were tested at Eglin AFB, Florida in late 1952. These Sabres were then rushed to Korea for combat tests with the 4th FIW. The first GUNVAL mission was flown in January of 1953. A third 'gun port' has been painted under the 20 MM muzzle ports to make the aircraft appear the same as other .50 caliber machine gun armed F-86s. (Paul Peterson)

(Above) A 15th TRS RF-86F sits in the snow at Kimpo in late 1953. The canopy was covered by a tarp, whose straps were attached to the nose gear and speed brake. At least three RF-86Fs were in service during the Korean War. Like the earlier RF-86As, RF-86Fs wore markings identical to those of the 4th FIW aircraft and flew as part of their fighter mission until the target area was reached. (Ralph Newman)

(Below) The Republic of Korea Air Force (ROKAF) received ten RF-86Fs when they were phased out of service with the USAF's 15th TRS. This 10th FW RF-86F carries the large 200 gallon (757 liter) combat drop tanks developed for the Sabre after the end of the Korean War. The aircraft was taxiing at Suwon on 8 May 1968. ROKAF Sabres were painted Silver to retard corrosion. (Stephen Miller)

(Above) Mr Ozzie Niedermann, the North American technical representative at Kimpo, perches on the wing of a factory-built RF-86F assigned to the 67th TRW in 1953. Gun 'ports' have been painted on the blast panel. The large bulge in the camera bay door covered the camera magazine of the vertically-mounted K-22 cameras. The 18 factory-built RF-86Fs featured the '6-3 hard wing'. (Ozzie Neidermann)

Mitsubishi converted eighteen F-86F-40s into RF-86Fs for the Japanese Air Self Defense Force from 1961 through 1962. These reconnaissance Sabres were patterned after USAF RF-86Fs. The small blade antenna on top of the nose was a Tactical Air Navigation (TACAN) unit. Machine gun 'ports' were painted on the nose as a deception measure. (Hideki Nagakubo)

The Federal German Bundesluftwaffe began receiving Canadair Sabre Mk 5s and 6s in December of 1957, initially assigning them to the fighter-interceptor role. GAF Sabres had AIM-9 Sidewinder air-to-air missiles (AAMs) added to their armament in 1959. This Sabre Mk 6 is from the 1st Staffel of JG-72 and was part of the escort flight for Adolph Galland on 'Sabre Night' held at Phalsbourg AB, France on 18 May 1962. Galland was a Luftwaffe fighter ace during World War Two. (James McLennan)

Several air forces around the world had aerobatic teams equipped with F-86 Sabres, with the Italian Air Force fielding three separate teams. This Canadair Sabre Mk 4 (F-86E) was part of the 'Cavallino Rampante' team. This team flew exhibitions throughout Europe during the late 1960s. The Sabre Mk 4 had the '6-3 hard wing' installed prior to delivery to Italy in 1956. (IAF)

The Royal Saudi Air Force began receiving the first of 16 F-86Fs in 1958, with all aircraft being ex-USAF airframes transferred from units in Europe. The Saudi aircraft arrived in natural metal finish before being painted overall Gray (FS 36231) with green markings. Saudi aircraft were brought up to F-86F-40 standard with the extended span '6-3 wing' and leading edge slats. This Sabre was assigned to No. 7 Squadron at Dhahran, Saudi Arabia in November of 1966. (Frank McDonald)

(Above) An F-86E-10 assigned to the 334th FIS at Kimpo gleams shortly after undergoing a major Inspect and Repair As Necessary (IRAN) overhaul at the Rear Echelon Maintenance Facility (REMCO) in Tsuiki, Japan in 1952. The external surfaces of the Sabre were polished during IRAN. This aircraft was flown by Capt Bill Lilley, a seven-victory ace with the 4th FIW during 1952. (Curt Francom)

(Below) Two 21st FBW F-86Fs depart George AFB, California in December of 1954 enroute to a European deployment. The Sabres deployed from George to Phalsbourg AB, France. The nose landing gear of the lead aircraft has already rotated back, turned 90°, and settled into the nose gear bay. (NAA)

(Above) It was unusual to see any aircraft outside of the US Air Force with personal markings of any kind, much less 'art'. This Chinese Nationalist Air Force F-86F painted with 'girlie art' was based at Chi-Yi AB, Taiwan in 1958. Part of the explanation for the artwork was that Chinese pilots flew these Sabres during the day and American pilots flew them at night. (Bill Van Dine)

(Right) Three F-86Fs from the 461st FDS cruise over Germany in 1956. The 86th FDW experimented with camouflage in 1956, painting several of their Sabres with Royal Air Force colors in a random pattern — no two aircraft were the same. The aircraft were painted Sea Gray and Dark Green on the upper surfaces with PRU Blue on the undersurfaces. All the standard USAF and squadron markings were then reapplied to the Sabres. The scheme was not adopted by the USAF. (via David Menard)

(Above) One of the 461st FDS F-86Fs cruises over Germany wearing the experimental Sea Gray and Dark Green camouflage applied in 1956. The scheme was never adopted, although experiments with both F-84Gs and F-86Fs proved this camouflage to be effective at low levels. Applying the paint reduced the Sabre's top speed by approximately 20 MPH (32.2 KMH). (Robb Satterfield)

(Below) Bee Gee's Bird was an F-86F assigned to the 310th FBS at Osan-ni AB, South Korea in January of 1958. An auxiliary power unit (APU) is parked behind the Sabre's port wing. This aircraft has been retrofitted with the extended span '6-3 hard wing' with leading edge slats. This wing was identical to the F-40 wing found on Japanese Air Self Defense Force Sabres. The extended span '6-3' wing increased the Sabre's low speed stability. (Bill Gregory)

(Above) An ex-RAF Sabre F.Mk 4 sits on the ramp at Practia de Marie AB, Italy in 1955. This aircraft has been given temporary USAF markings and painted in a camouflage of gloss Sea Gray and Dark Green over PRU Blue. Three hundred and one Canadair-built Sabre F.Mk 4s were sold to Italy and Yugoslavia following their service with the RAF. The F.Mk 4s had the '6-3 hard wing' installed. These Sabres were redesignated F-86E(M) by the USAF prior to delivery to another country. (Gary Sparks)

FEAF Recognition Markings

1950 - 1951
(4th FIG Only)

1951 - 1953
(All Units)

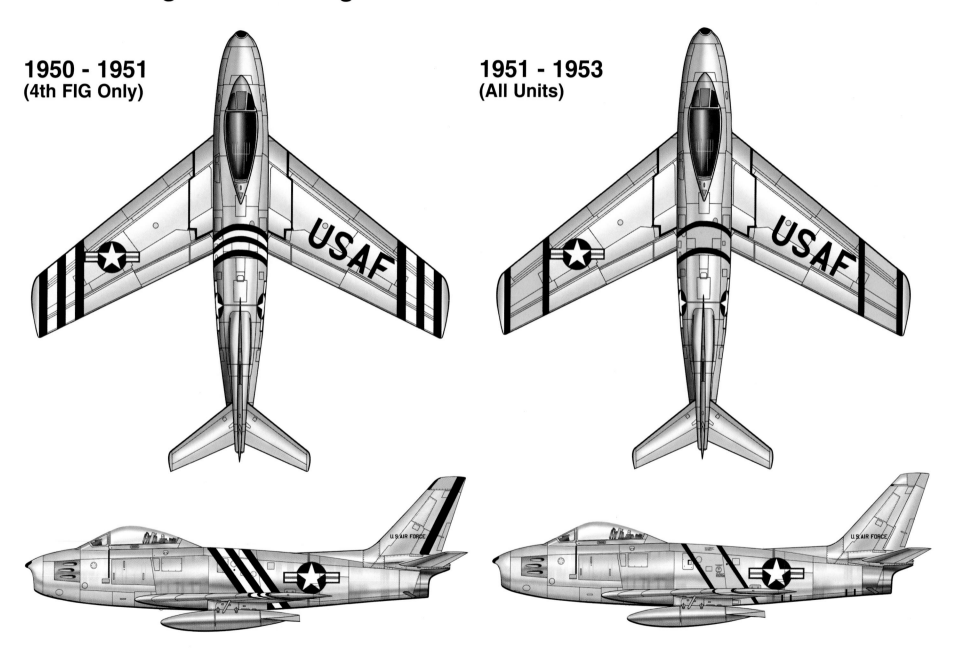

Sabre pilots of the 39th FIS prepare for their missions in the equipment room at Suwon. The P3 pilot helmets hanging from the ceiling display a variety of personal markings. The pilot in the foreground is an Royal Air Force exchange officer whose White helmet displays the RAF roundel — red center, white inner ring, and blue outer ring. His survival equipment includes a 'Mae West' life preserver, a .45 caliber pistol, and a knife. The pilot on the right is zipping up the anti-G suit 'chaps' (later known as 'speed jeans') worn by Sabre pilots in Korea. (USAF)

Col Robert Baldwin flew Nina V, an F-86F, while commanding the 51st FIW at Suwon in 1953. Col Baldwin, an ace with five victories, wears the typical fighter pilot garb in Korea. Pilots wore flight suits in either Olive Drab, Khaki, or Dark Blue. Sabre pilots additionally wore an Olive anti-G suit, an Olive Green or Dark Blue L-2B jacket with Yellow 'Mae West' life preserver, and an Olive Green parachute pack. The anti-G suit constricted a pilot's blood flow at the legs and waist during hard maneuvers to prevent him from losing consciousness. (USAF)

(Above) Virginia Belle/GOPHER PATROL was an F-86E assigned to the 335th FIS at Kimpo in 1952. This Sabre carries a 120 gallon (454.2 liter) drop tank under the starboard wing. Virginia Belle was used for combat testing of the Sabre as a fighter-bomber. Col Walker (Bud) Mahurin, a WW II ace, was shot down on 13 May 1952 while flying an F-86 fighter-bomber mission and became a prisoner of war. The later F-86F mounted four underwing pylons to carry both bombs and a pair of drop tanks. (NAA)

(Below) Ground crewmen refuel a Yellow-tailed F-86F-35 assigned to the 493rd FBS, 48th FBW, at Dhahran, Saudi Arabia on 30 January 1955. This Sabre was participating in OPERATION MORNING STAR, which sent US air power to Saudi Arabia. The F-86F was equipped with fuel filler caps on both sides of the fuselage and on both wings. The F-35 was the only F-86F variant capable of delivering nuclear weapons. An RCAF Sabre Mk 5 is parked in the background. (USAF)

(Above) Lt Col George Ruddell marks his fifth MiG-15 kill in the machine gun residue on his F-86F, MIG MAD MAVIS, after returning to Suwon on 18 May 1953. The gun residue pattern was typical of F-86s after their .50 caliber M3 machine guns had been fired. Col Ruddell, commander of the 39th FIS, finished the Korean War with eight MiG kills. Capt Joseph McConnell scored his 16th victory on this date and became the Korean War's top American air ace. (Author)

F-86 Pilot (circa 1952)

(Above) Lt Col George Ruddell of the 39th FIS, 51st FIW poses beside his F-86F MIG MAD MAVIS in April of 1953. Ruddell is wearing the typical clothing of a fighter pilot in Korea, including the type A2 leather flight jacket and newer type P4 helmet with flip-up visor. Additionally, Ruddell wears an orange 'Mae West' life preserver. The black oxygen mask and hose are attached to the left shoulder strap of Ruddell's jacket. (USAF)

(Left) 1/Lt Earl Wisecarver adjusts his helmet strap before entering this F-86F, THE HUFF, prior to another mission to 'MiG Alley' during the summer of 1953. THE HUFF was normally flown by Lt Jim Thompson. Although pilots had 'assigned' aircraft, they often flew whatever aircraft was available in order to get credit for another mission. A tour of duty in Korea was 100 missions, although this was extended by an additional 25 missions if conditions warranted. (Dean Abbott)

(Above) A pair of 4th FIW F-86s sit on the ramp at K-14 in April of 1952. The 4th FIW had changed their FEAF identification stripes from black and white to yellow and black by this date. No tail markings were carried by the Wing's Sabres at this time. The near aircraft is Lt Martin Bambrick's F-86A, while the far aircraft is Capt Bob Love's BERNIE'S BO. Capt Love shot down six MiGs in this F-86E while assigned to the 335th FIS. (Martin Bambrick)

(Below) LITTLE BUTCH, an F-86E assigned to the 335th FIS, 4th FIW, is towed along the ramp at K-14. The painted identification stripes have peeled away due to the Sabre being constantly flown at speeds approaching Mach One. The five red star victory marks on the starboard side under the cockpit symbolize victories credited to the aircraft while being flown by various pilots. This style of markings was a 4th FIW tradition. (Don Prouty)

Canadair Ltd built a large number of Sabres for different air forces, including the Royal Canadian Air Force, RAF, West German Luftwaffe, and the US Air Force. This aircraft is a Sabre Mk 2, a license-built version of the F-86E-1. Canadair built a total of 352 Sabre Mk 2s, including 60 that served with the US Air Force in Korea under the designation F-86E-6. This RCAF Sabre Mk 2 served with No. 434 Squadron at Zweibrücken, West Germany in 1954. (RCAF)

The Chinese Nationalist Air Force aerobatic team 'Thunder Tigers' made this close formation pass during EXERCISE SKY SOLDIER IV held on Taiwan in October of 1963. Taiwanese Sabres were all drawn from US Far East assets and brought up to the latest standards. These standards included installation of the extended span '6-3' wing with leading edge slats and AIM-9 Sidewinder air-to-air missile (AAM) capability. Taiwanese F-86s claimed 29 Chinese MiG-17 kills over the Formosa Straits in August of 1958. (USAF)

This Canadair Sabre F.Mk 4 served with the 4ª Aerobrigata, Italian Air Force in 1957. The 428 Sabre F.Mk 4s were transferred to Italy and Yugoslavia following service with the RAF under the Mutual Defense Assistance Pact (MDAP). The Sabre Mk. 4 (designated Sabre F.Mk 4 in RAF service) was a copy of the F-86E-10, with the '6-3 hard wing' installed prior to delivery to Italy in 1956. Italian Sabres were camouflaged Dark Green and Sea Gray with PRU Blue undersurfaces. (IAF)

North American Aviation and Mitsubishi Heavy Industries built a total of 480 F-86Fs between 1955 and 1961 — primarily for the Japanese Air Self Defense Force. Forty-five of the North American-built aircraft were returned by Japan in 1959. Most of the JASDF Sabre force were F-86F-40s with the extended '6-3' wing with leading edge slats. The aircraft were painted overall Silver to retard corrosion. This aircraft was assigned to the 7th FS at Komatsu in May of 1974. (Jim Sullivan)

During the mid-1950s, the Royal Canadian Air Force adopted a camouflage scheme of Sea Gray and Dark Green with PRU Blue undersurfaces. This Canadair Sabre Mk. 6 was assigned to No. 430 Squadron based at Grostenquin, France in 1963. The Sabre Mk. 6 used an F-86F air frame, powered by a Canadian-built Orenda 10 engine. These Sabres were also equipped with a slatted '6-3, short span' wing. (via Joe Bruch)

The Australian Sabre was different from any USAF F-86 variant. The Commonwealth CA-26 Sabre was powered by a Rolls-Royce Avon RA-7 engine providing 7500 LBS (3402 KG) of thrust — 1550 LBS (703 KG) greater thrust than that provided by the F-86F's General Electric J47 engine. The engine installation required a three-inch (7.6 CM) spread of the intake area to provide air for the deeper breathing Avon engine. The CA-26 was armed with two 30 MM Aden cannons and two AIM-9 Sidewinder AAMs. (Mike Fox)

The Republic of Korea Air Force (ROK) aerobatic team flew this F-86F in 1963. The team's aircraft had red, white, and blue noses with blue and white tail checks, plus the black and yellow identification bands applied to all Sabres in Korea. This aircraft was a standard F-86F-30 modified with the extended span '6-3' wing with leading edge slats. (Merle Olmsted)

The Federal German Bundesluftwaffe was equipped with Canadair Sabre Mk 5s and Mk 6s from 1957 to 1968. Two Sabre Mk 6s of JG-71 are parked at Leeuwarden, Netherlands in September of 1961 — one in camouflage and the other in natural metal finish. The tulip nose and tail design were applied in recognition of JG-71's commander, World War II Luftwaffe ace Erich Hartmann. The tulip was Hartmann's personal emblem during World War Two when he shot down 352 enemy aircraft. (Merle Olmsted)

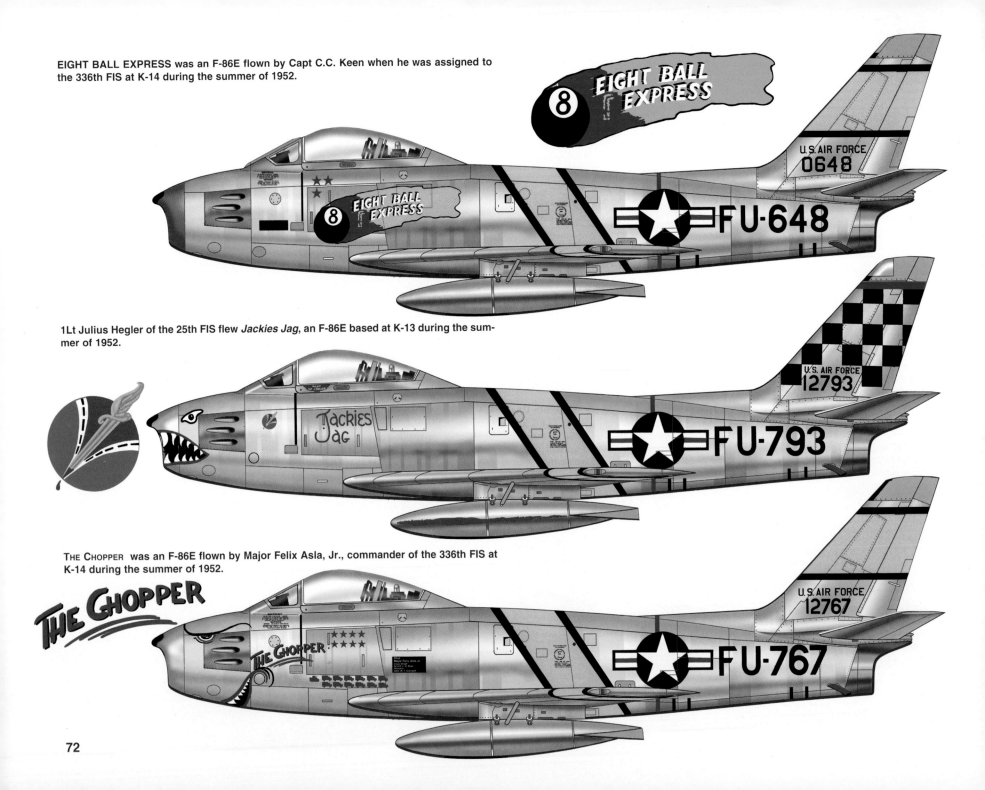

EIGHT BALL EXPRESS was an F-86E flown by Capt C.C. Keen when he was assigned to the 336th FIS at K-14 during the summer of 1952.

1Lt Julius Hegler of the 25th FIS flew *Jackies Jag*, an F-86E based at K-13 during the summer of 1952.

THE CHOPPER was an F-86E flown by Major Felix Asla, Jr., commander of the 336th FIS at K-14 during the summer of 1952.

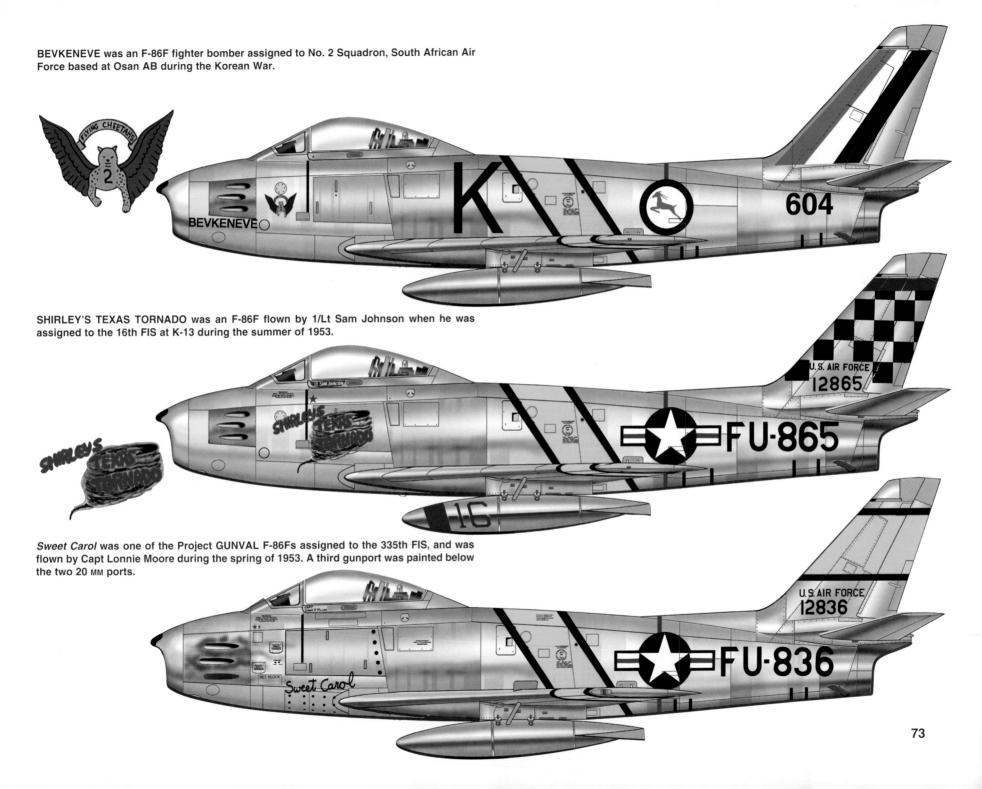

BEVKENEVE was an F-86F fighter bomber assigned to No. 2 Squadron, South African Air Force based at Osan AB during the Korean War.

SHIRLEY'S TEXAS TORNADO was an F-86F flown by 1/Lt Sam Johnson when he was assigned to the 16th FIS at K-13 during the summer of 1953.

Sweet Carol was one of the Project GUNVAL F-86Fs assigned to the 335th FIS, and was flown by Capt Lonnie Moore during the spring of 1953. A third gunport was painted below the two 20 mm ports.

JUST JOAN, an F-86F assigned to No. 2 Squadron, SAAF, undergoes a tire change at Osan-Ni (K-55), Korea in the spring of 1953. The aircraft sits on jack stands while a crew chief uses an air wrench to tighten the wheel bolts. Canvas covers over the cockpit and wings were normally used anytime the Sabre was not flying. (SAAF)

KARENS KART was initially assigned to Lt Col Al Kelly, the commander of the 51st Fighter Interceptor Group (FIG) at Suwon in 1952. The aircraft was then flown by Col Bob Baldwin, who succeeded Col Kelly as Group CO. A fighter group was the combat arm of a fighter wing at that time. Col Kelly scored 2.5 victories in Korea. The red, yellow, and blue stripes on the nose signify the squadron colors of the 51st FIG. (Herb Goldstein)

This unusual piece of equipment, a bright red parasol, was not supplied by North American or the USAF. The parasol was used to keep the sun off the cockpit of MIG MAD MARINE/*LYN ANNIE DAVE* I, an F-86F assigned to the 25th FIS at Suwon in 1953. Major John Glenn, USMC, future astronaut and Senator, scored three victories in this aircraft while on 'loan' to the 51st FIW. (Bob Baldwin)

An F-86E from the 25th FIS, 51st FIW jettisons a pair of the Japanese-built 120 gallon (454.2 liter) drop tanks prior to engaging MiG-15s over the Yalu River in 1952. The Japanese tanks had a tendency to 'ride up' over the top of the wing and damage the leading edge slats if the pilot was careless. These tanks were usually painted Olive Drab as a quick identification measure. (USAF)

(Above) A 4th FIW crewman refuels Dottie, Col Donald Hall's F-86F, on the ramp at K-14 during the summer of 1953. Aircraft in Korea were always kept fully fueled to retard condensation caused by the extreme weather conditions. The drop tanks will be hung and filled just prior to the aircraft going on a five-minute alert or before the next mission. Col Hall was Commander of the 4th FIW during the latter half of 1953. (USAF)

(Below) The crew chief checks with Captain Cecil Foster prior to 'engine start' for another mission from the soggy parking ramp at K-13 in 1952. Capt Foster scored a total of nine victories with the 16th FIS. A Boeing B-29 undergoing repairs on the ramp was almost a normal occurrence, due to the MiGs causing havoc for the Superfortresses even when the B-29s had F-86 escorts. (NAA)

(Above) The years, the units, and the colors changed, but the Korean weather stayed the same. Judy Ann was an F-86F assigned to the 58th FBG at Osan-ni during the latter half of 1957. Although many Sabres stationed in Korea had been fitted with the '6-3, extended span wing' with slats by this time, Judy was not yet retrofitted. (R.B. Ochs)

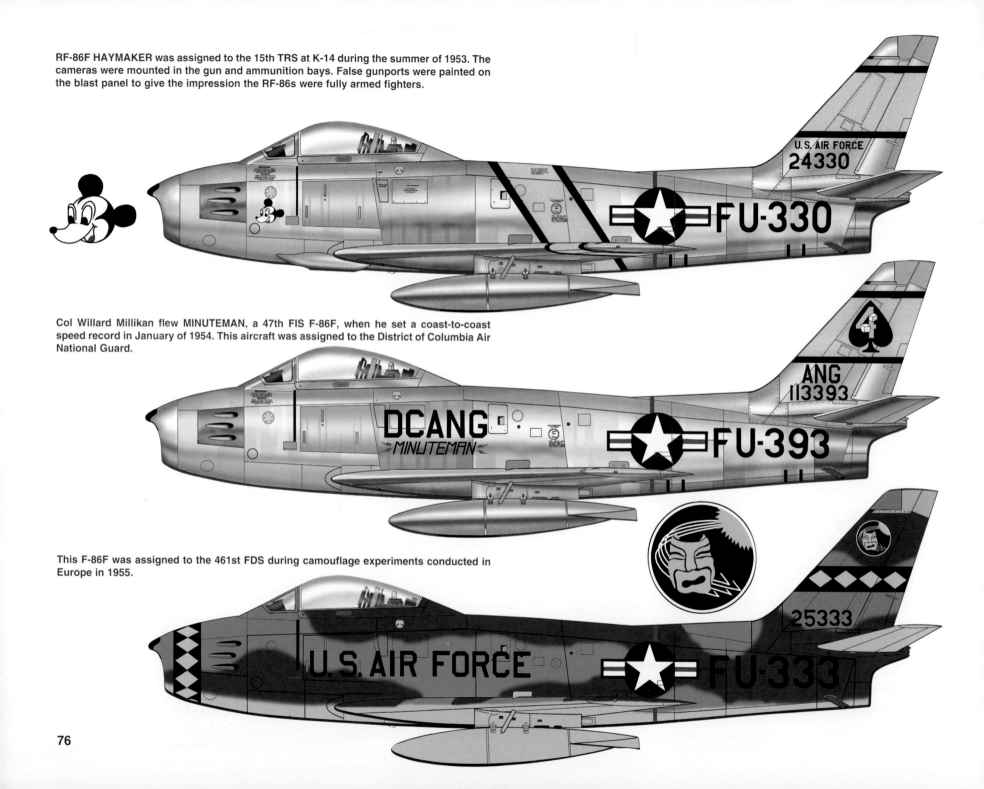

RF-86F HAYMAKER was assigned to the 15th TRS at K-14 during the summer of 1953. The cameras were mounted in the gun and ammunition bays. False gunports were painted on the blast panel to give the impression the RF-86s were fully armed fighters.

U.S. AIR FORCE
24330
FU-330

Col Willard Millikan flew MINUTEMAN, a 47th FIS F-86F, when he set a coast-to-coast speed record in January of 1954. This aircraft was assigned to the District of Columbia Air National Guard.

ANG
113393
DCANG
MINUTEMAN
FU-393

This F-86F was assigned to the 461st FDS during camouflage experiments conducted in Europe in 1955.

25333
U.S. AIR FORCE
FU-333

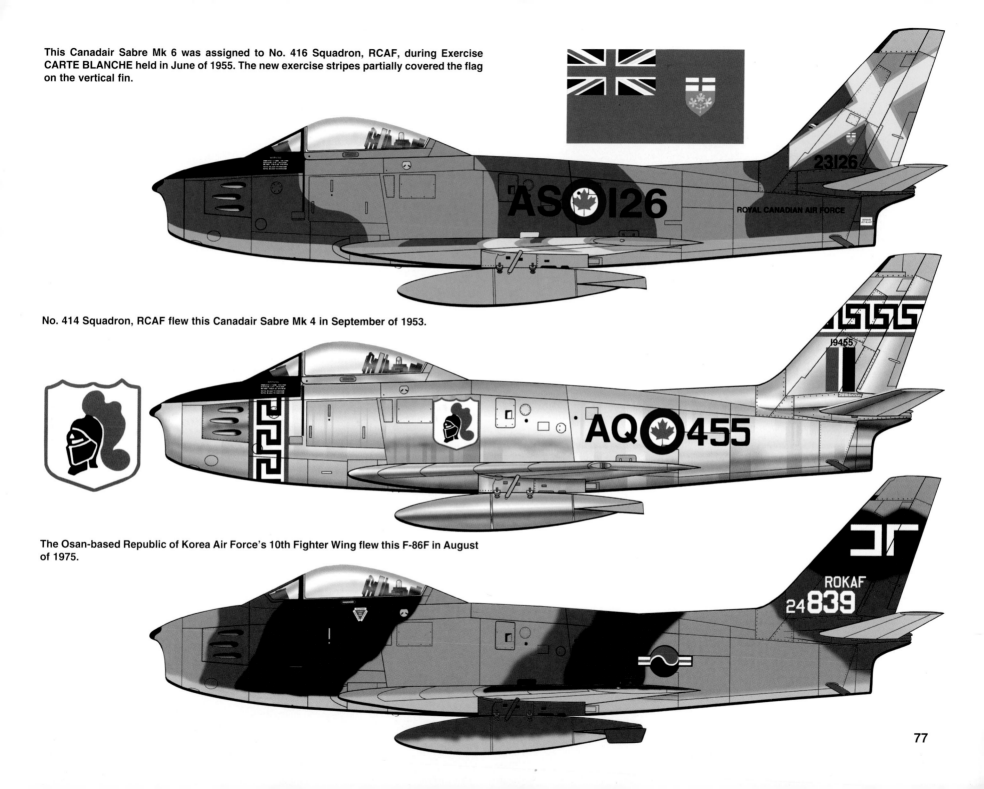

This Canadair Sabre Mk 6 was assigned to No. 416 Squadron, RCAF, during Exercise CARTE BLANCHE held in June of 1955. The new exercise stripes partially covered the flag on the vertical fin.

No. 414 Squadron, RCAF flew this Canadair Sabre Mk 4 in September of 1953.

The Osan-based Republic of Korea Air Force's 10th Fighter Wing flew this F-86F in August of 1975.

77

MR. BONES "V" was the F-86E flown by Major W.W. 'Bones' Marshall when he commanded the 335th FIS at K-14 in 1952. 'Bones' was one of the early F-86E-1s with the light gray fiberglass intake. The cockpit side panel shows Maj Marshall's total score with victories on top (seven), 'probables' in the second row (one half), and 'damaged' in the bottom row (five). (Bones Marshall)

Col Bob Baldwin leads 'Tiger Flight', 25th FIS, for a MiG sweep in the spring of 1953. His aircraft, NINA II (on left), was an F-86E-10 and the former mount of Lt Col Al Kelly. Col Baldwin is flying a Confederate flag from the cockpit. Both the main and nose wheel doors are retracted — a normal occurrence when the engine was running and hydraulic pressure had built up. Col Baldwin scored five victories in the Korean War in various aircraft, all named NINA. (Hank Buttlemann)

The only pilot to achieve 'ace' status who was not assigned to a fighter-interceptor unit in Korea was Major James Hagerstrom. He scored eight victories while flying with the 67th Fighter Bomber Squadron at Osan-ni in 1953. Maj Hagerstrom's F-86F was named "MIG POISON" and was decorated with a large skull and crossbones on the gun bay door. (Don McNamara)

The third highest scoring ace with the 4th FIG was Col Royal Baker, who scored 13 victories while commanding the Group in 1952. Col Baker's aircraft, Angel Face & The Babes/THE KING, was an F-86E assigned to the 336th FIS at K-14. Highly polished finishes were not normal in Korea due to the weather and combat taking their toll on the aircraft finish. Col Baker, however, was the boss! (NAA)

(Above) Captain Manuel J. 'Pete' Fernandez returns to Kimpo on 16 May 1953 minus drop tanks and with soot stained gun ports. He had just shot down another MiG-15, bringing his score to 14.5 victories. This total made Fernandez the third-highest scoring ace in the 4th FIW. 'Pete' flew with the 334th FIS in 1953. (USAF)

(Right) The American 'Ace of Aces' in Korea was Captain Joseph McConnell, who scored 16 victories flying with the 39th FIS at Suwon in 1953. 'Mac' scored three MiG kills on 18 May to bring his total to 16. McConnell was promptly grounded and sent home as the first 'triple ace' in Korea. After he had landed, his aircraft was hurriedly repainted with 16 red stars and a misspelled name — BEAUTIOUS BUTCH II became BEAUTEOUS BUTCH II on the port side. His mother's name, BETTY, remained unaltered on the starboard side. This Sabre was an F-86F-1 retrofitted with a '6-3 hard wing' kit. (NAA)

Aircraft, Armor, and Warships

1169 La 5/7 Fighters

1170 Fw 190

1171 de Havilland DH 2

5518 F/A-18 Hornet

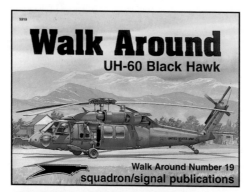

5519 UH-60 Black Hawk

5520 Space Shuttle

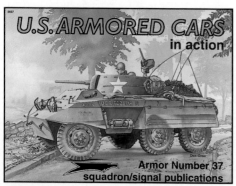

2037 U.S. Armored Cars

2038 U.S. Self-Propelled Guns

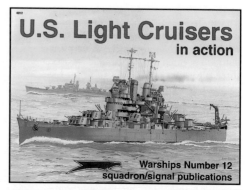

4012 U.S. Light Cruisers

from squadron/signal publications